U0102058

UP AND OUT OF POVERTY

XI JINPING

UP AND OUT OF POVERTY

POVERTY

Selected Speeches and Writings from Fujian

 THE SECRETARIAT OF THE CHINESE FOLLOW-UP COMMITTEE
OF THE FORUM ON CHINA-AFRICA COOPERATION

 FOREIGN LANGUAGES PRESS

 FUJIAN PEOPLE'S PUBLISHING HOUSE

First Edition 2016
Sixth Printing 2019

ISBN 978-7-119-10556-7
© Foreign Languages Press Co., Ltd.
The Secretariat of the Chinese Follow-up Committee
of the Forum on China-Africa Cooperation
Fujian People's Publishing House Co., Ltd., 2016

Published by Foreign Languages Press Co., Ltd.,
Fujian People's Publishing House Co., Ltd.
24 Baiwanzhuang Road, Beijing 100037, China
http://www.flp.com.cn
Email: flp@CIPG.org.cn

Distributed by China International Book Trading Corporation
35 Chegongzhuang Xilu, Beijing 100044, China
P.O. Box 399, Beijing, China
Printed in the People's Republic of China

Attending a meeting for the Party committee and government of Shouning County on April 30, 1990.

Leading local officials of Ningde Prefecture to participate in a volunteer project on December 2, 1989.

Handling official business on a fact-finding mission in Xiadang Township, Shouning County, on July 19, 1989.

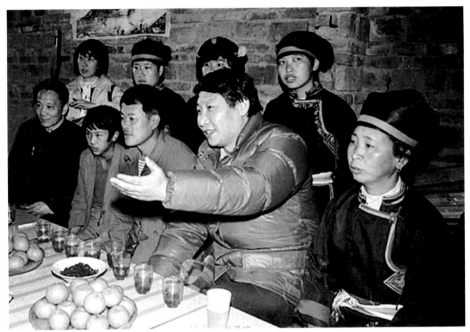

Talking to villagers of ethnic minority in Jiuxian Village, Jiudu Township, Ningde Prefecture, on January 18, 1989.

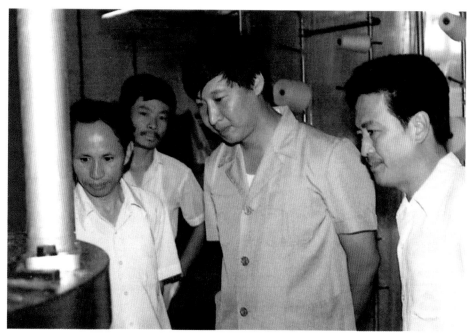

Conducting an investigation about the industrial development in Xiapu County on August 10, 1988.

With prefecture and county leaders in a mountain village of Shouning County in July 1989.

Visiting retired officials and listening to their suggestions in January 1989.

Successful oyster farming using the hanging-net method in Gongyu Village, Zhangwan Town, Ningde Prefecture.

Rich forest resources in Ningde.

Paddy fields in Ningde.

Foreword[1]

Xiang Nan[2]

The nine counties and cities of Ningde Prefecture constitute one of Fujian's more impoverished regions. Even though I visited all of those counties when I worked in Fujian, I always regretted not being able to help Ningde Prefecture more than I was able to at the time.

I was greatly inspired while recently reading some of the speeches and articles written by my colleague Xi Jinping while he was working in Ningde Prefecture. I have also been fortunate enough to revisit several counties in that region lately where I was very excited to see that the people there no longer have to worry about daily necessities, the economy is thriving, and the leadership of the prefectural committee of the Communist Party of China is in high spirits. All of this to a certain extent makes up for what I was unable to accomplish.

During their nearly two years working in Ningde, Xi Jinping and the departments under his leadership took the lead in implementing their "four grassroots initiatives."[3] Their detailed inspections and informed considerations of Ningde's own characteristics and history allowed them to make proposals firmly rooted in the local situation. They thoroughly did away with the current bad leadership habits of grandiose, empty, and formulaic speech. Even though after he moved on to new posts from Ningde, there is no doubt that the good conduct Xi Jinping practiced has been an inspiration to his successors, as what exists today comes from the past.

The strongest feature of Xi Jinping's writing from this period is that it never strays from the focus of economic development. This focus has become even clearer after Deng Xiaoping's speeches given during his recent south China inspection tour. This was not always the case, however, and for quite a long time some people had different opinions. Prefectures, counties, cities, departments, and enterprises certainly faced daunting workloads, and some people often – consciously or unconsciously – focused their attention on tasks other than economic development in order to showcase their other achievements. Some of these tasks were undoubtedly quite important, but nevertheless we still had to take economic development, and not any other issue, as our ultimate goal. Too many unrelated objectives will necessarily weaken the central focus of economic development. Xi Jinping once saw that a town government office he was visiting had a wall covered in red banners with congratulations for all sorts of accomplishments except for economic development. Xi thought that while it was certainly great to be awarded such honor banners, the leadership could not elevate relatively minor tasks without focusing on the main objective. He called for everyone to join forces to make full use of the geographical advantages Ningde was blessed with and form an "economic chorus," not another central task. Under his plan, Ningde firmly adhered to the principle of "one central task, two basic points"[4] at all times.

With Ningde's relative poverty in mind, Xi Jinping repeatedly called for bold reforms and opening up. Even though Ningde is somewhat economically disadvantaged, it lies in a coastal region right next to Taiwan and the Pacific Ocean, and it has one of China's few deep-water ports. Given these features, the fastest way to resolve the persistent problems of lack of funding and talent is to speed up reforms, open up even further, increase domestic cooperation, and absorb foreign investment. We must not shy away from using outside funds and technology to develop our own resources, including Ningde's unique marine, stone, and lumber resources. This requires greater awareness of reform and opening up among officials and better business sense. No difficulty is too great as long as we are bold enough, try new things, and act first. With bolder reforms and opening up, the economy may pick up even faster, and there will be hope for lifting the region out of poverty and creating wealth.

Xi Jinping has thought deeply and carefully about many issues. He is a strong proponent of the theory of "water droplets drilling through rock" and "letting the weak hatchling be the first to fly" to encourage people to be fearless pioneers and thoroughly do away with formalism and false appearances. He wants officials to truly keep the people in their hearts. We have always believed that poverty is not something to be feared, and we should be most on guard against rushing ahead without thought and spirit. If all we do is want those above us to bail us out and complain about our unfair lot in life, how will we ever be able to eliminate poverty? We must free our mind and get down to real work. Our work must be performed one step at a time, and our experience will accumulate one step at a time. As long as we look to ourselves for the answers and become self-reliant, we will be able to cast off our fetters and move forward with ease. With persistence, even water droplets can drill through stone. Short-term projects with quick results can be great for poverty alleviation, but we cannot let ourselves be content with these and only focus on the short-term. The work of poverty alleviation is a long-term task. Impoverished regions cannot make economic, societal, and environmental advances without the mindset of the Foolish Old Man Who Removed the Mountains[5] and the "foolish" work of trying to tame rivers and mountains, we will never emerge from poverty and backwardness.

The success or failure of all work in the region is determined by the ambitions, thinking, and the working practices of those young officials in important positions who are trying to improve their backward areas. They must fully use their brains, dare to explore, and boldly push their work forward. Even if some ideas are not completely in line with the local situation and some methods may not produce immediate results, we must not be panic. Nobody can be perfect in everything they say or do. In this sense, Xi Jinping is no exception. The officials in our local prefectures, cities, counties, and townships can gain much insight from this pamphlet.

Notes

[1] The text was taken from the foreword to the Chinese edition.

[2] A native of Liancheng, Fujian Province, Xiang Nan (1918-1997) worked to establish revolutionary base areas in the border regions of Fujian, Zhejiang, and Jiangxi provinces. He arrived at the Yancheng headquarters of the New Fourth Army in the spring of 1941. After the founding of the People's Republic of China in 1949, he served as secretary of the Communist Youth League of Anhui Province, secretary of the East China Bureau of the Communist Youth League, secretary of the Youth League Central Committee, the first secretary of the Fujian Provincial Party Committee, and the first political commissar of the Provincial Military Region. He served as chairman of the China Foundation for Poverty Alleviation from 1989 and later became its chief consultant.

[3] The "four grassroots initiatives" encouraged leading officials to investigate complaints and listen to ideas at the grassroots level; to go down to the grassroots to handle official business on the spot; to work with the grassroots to conduct research and investigations; and to go down to the grassroots to publicize the Party's guiding principles and policies. Xi Jinping strongly advocated for these initiatives in 1988, while he was working in Ningde, Fujian Province.

[4] "One central task, two basic points" are the basis of the Party line to guide policymaking during the primary stage of socialism. "One central task" refers to economic development; "two basic points" refer to the Four Cardinal Principles and the reform and opening-up policy.

[5] Source of English translation: Mao Zedong, "The Foolish Old Man Who Removed the Mountains," in *Selected Works of Mao Tsetung*, vol. 3 (Beijing: Foreign Languages Press, 1965), 321. – *Tr.*

CONTENTS

CONTENTS

How Can a Weak Hatchling Bird Be the First to Fly?

– Thoughts from Inspecting the Nine Counties of Ningde

September 1988

Impoverished Ningde Prefecture is undoubtedly just a "weak hatchling bird" in the vast space for developing the commodity economy. I arrived in Ningde in June to take up my new post, and from early July to early August several of my colleagues joined me in a tour of nine counties of Ningde as well as neighboring Wenzhou, Cangnan, and Yueqing in southern Zhejiang Province. As we visited, contemplated, and studied, our thoughts never strayed far from this question: in developing a commodity production economy in which "fish can leap at will in a boundless sea and birds can soar free beneath the limitless sky,"[1] can this "hatchling bird" of Ningde be the first to fly, and how can we make it so?

1. Being the first to "take flight"

Ningde is almost a world to itself – hard to get to, little information from the outside world, and an economy based on small-scale farming. Its commodity economy has developed even more sluggishly than other impoverished regions. When you mention Ningde, five words come to people's minds: "old, ethnic minority, remote, island, impoverished." In such a place that so much resembles a weak hatchling bird, how can we even dare to think about being the first to "take flight"? In my eyes, not only can we talk about it, we must loudly proclaim it. Impoverished regions cannot have impoverished ideals. "Being at peace with our lot," "finding contentment in poverty," "waiting for government aid, relying on financial grants, requiring poverty allowances," blaming everyone but ourselves – all of these concepts must be swept out with the trash. The weak hatchling bird can be the first to fly, and the poorest can be the first to become rich. But to be the first to "take flight" or to "become rich," we must first have such a concept in mind. Therefore, I believe that the most pressing task at the moment is for our Party members, officials, and people to free their minds, update their thinking, and tell everyone that the "weak hatchling bird can be the first to take flight and the poorest can be the first to become rich." This will allow us to break through old ways of looking at problems and do things in a positive frame of mind.

Many of our colleagues put their hopes in the state allocating more funds and arranging for more raw materials in their planning. Like General Han Xin's need for soldiers, the more the better. Generally speaking, it isn't a bad thing to have someone watching over you. This mindset is understandable, but we must also get one thing straight: we must see ourselves as the key to resolving shortages of raw materials and funds, and this changing responsibility is the prime concept of being the first to "take flight." We must not look to others for the answers to all of our problems, but rather to ourselves. For example, we can look to uncovering potential and reducing costs; we can build a stable network for material assistance through seeking domestic cooperation and foreign investment; and we can encourage counties to formulate preferential policies. There is no reason why impoverished regions cannot make extraordinary gains in unconfined areas and areas to their advantage. That is to say, it is entirely possible for impoverished regions to rely on their own efforts, policies, strengths, and advantages in certain areas to be the first to "take flight," and make up for the disadvantages brought about by poverty.

There is no dearth of examples of this. While many major electronics companies in large cities and even in special economic zones suffer from excessive capacity and find it difficult to pick up their operations, our impoverished region Xiapu continually produces its own electronic massage devices and special medical devices for men. They are in high demand with good reputation in China and overseas. Clearly, we cannot say that Xiapu has better conditions than the large cities and special economic zones, nor can we say that its industrial environment is better than what other major electronics companies have. This only goes to show that not only is it possible to be the first to "take flight," it is realistic. To impoverished regions, the concepts of commodities, markets, and competition are entirely new, and they all should be integral factors of wanting to be the first to "take flight." Without understanding these concepts, no matter how loudly we shout about it, the commodity economy will fall flat.

Here I want to especially emphasize the notion of building a commodity economy, and we cannot completely separate politics from economy. The five leading departments of all counties must arrange their own departmental work based on developing the economy. We must have an "economic chorus." It has already been ten years since the Third Plenary Session of the 11th CPC Central Committee made the decision to shift the focus of the Party's work onto economic development. But many of our colleagues still "act like they don't see what is right in front of their eyes"[2] when they encounter specific problems and cannot differentiate what is primary from what is secondary. Economic development is our primary theme, and the economy cannot be developed without us bearing it in mind day and night. Many of our township colleagues said that non-economic work has taken up most of their energy, and I believe that we must quickly put a stop to this. Most of the energy and time of township officials must be spent on economic work.

The coastal province of Guangdong was one of the first to open up, and it acted quickly and made brilliant achievements. The most important thing was that everyone throughout Guangdong wanted to be the first to "take flight," and with such a strong desire, they were eventually able to fly.

2. Flying across the sea

Once we can fly, of course we must strive to fly across the sea, weather the storms of the international market, and live through commodity economy in the world.

Of the four coastal counties of our prefecture, Ningde and Xiapu counties have been on the list of opening-up counties, and Fu'an and Fuding are doing everything they can to get on the list. The first two counties already have basic policies for opening up. Of course, this only shows the direction we are going in, and whether or not we can keep on opening up will depend on our own work. We must clearly recognize this and have a sense of urgency.

How do we develop the opening-up counties? This is a general question. Due to differences in time, location, and production factors, the models of opening up will be varied, and we cannot simply copy the methods used by special economic zones or opening-up cities. We must forge our own suitable path based on our own actual situation. Opening up requires a process of preparation such as improving the investment environment, creating conditions for foreign exchange earnings, and making more products that can be sold overseas.

Let's take the investment environment as an example. Even though we cannot compete with cities and developed regions in terms of "water, power, gas, roads, and bridges," we can at least get off to a good start. Some say that we have to start over from scratch, but I disagree. We must come up with our strategy based on the regional situation and regional strengths. We must rely on the current layout of our cities and towns, and we cannot depart from our current urban living facilities to start over and build a new development zone. This might work in other places, but not in our prefecture. The reason is simple: our finances simply won't support such a plan.

Since we lack "hardware," we can turn to "software." There is much we can do in building our soft environment. Foreign companies that invest in China complain the most about poor efficiency, too many authorities, and authorities passing the buck all too often. If we look at general conditions such as input, output, and cost, our prefecture cannot rival other places. But this is all the more reason to build our soft environment. Such "software" effort is a superb technique that "weak hatchling" impoverished regions can use to soar across the sea. We should not imitate the big cities and set up giant institutions, but rather take a completely new approach from the beginning. For example, we can simplify procedures, reduce fees, improve the quality of service, and go through one-stop registration at "one window and with one official stamp," and so on. Furthermore, while resolutely following national laws and regulations, we can also focus on the local situation and consider formulating our own rules and regulations that offer genuine protection of the legitimate rights and interests of foreign companies. Without a sense of security, foreign companies will not come, and those who are already here will leave. I must remind everyone here that we cannot turn foreign-invested enterprises into state-operated enterprises. We must truly allow foreign companies to have their own production management that follows international norms.

We will know that our "software" effort has succeeded, and we will be able to fly across the sea after our message gets out and we start seeing people willing to travel the rugged terrain for hundreds of miles to come to our impoverished region, begin investing, and start setting up businesses.

3. The bird fills out with strong wings

To make the weak hatchling bird be the first to take flight, fly fast, and fly high, we must explore a local path suitable for economic development.

The key to what kind of development path Ningde takes lies in how the wheels of agriculture and industry turn.

Ningde mainly relies on agriculture for a living, and while we are poor because of agriculture, we can also only become rich through agriculture as well. The small farming economy cannot make one rich, nor does it have much of a future. Instead, we must turn to "big agriculture." That is, agriculturally, "on the mountain one lives off the mountain, and by the sea one lives off the sea." While guaranteeing food production, we must rely on mountains, seas and paddy fields, develop rural enterprises, and have an all-round development of agriculture, forestry, livestock, side-line products, and fishery. To "live off the mountain," we must look to forestry, tea, and fruit. "The forest grows as soon as the land is set aside."[3] In Zhouning County, Huang Zhenfang's family has a nice forest that has provided us with some ideas for developing forestry industry. Our prefecture has a great advantage in producing tealeaves, and it accounts for 1/4 of all production in the province. Currently, per-hectare yield is low, and our main efforts should be on increasing the per-unit yield while also focusing on rebuilding old tea plantations. There is also a great future in fruit planting, and in particular we should greatly develop the fruit that Ningde specializes in, such as the late-maturing lychees in Xiapu and Ningde, four-season pomelos of Fuding, Furong plums of Fu'an, and Younai plums of Gutian. To "live off the sea," apart from continuing marine fishing, tidal-flat aquaculture also has potential and can increase per-unit yield. The key to developing tidal-flat aquaculture is how the feed industry can meet the demand of aquaculture farms. Township enterprises are important pillars of the rural collective economy, and they should take advantage of local conditions, that is, the need to process and utilize agricultural and side-line products. Labor-intensive enterprises that serve large urban industries should mostly be collectively run to absorb much of the surplus labor force, and the rural industry structure should be properly adjusted to let more farmers get on the path toward prosperity.

Industry is the driving force for developing our prefecture. For industry, the relationship between speed and benefits must be properly handled: both must be firmly focused, and one cannot be neglected for the other. Once the benefits start to come in, the speed can be increased, and this is the only way to quickly shrink the gap between it and other cities. We must develop industry using local resources, but we also should not blindly oppose starting new projects. We can start projects as soon as opportunities present themselves. As long as there are good benefits from the investments and loans and as long as the products can be sold well on the market, we should also consider developing the processing industry with non-local resources. Of course, we should not start any project that doesn't deliver good benefits, and we must absolutely not allow the short-term behavior of blindly starting projects just to acquire officialdom vanity. We must emphasize the benefits of economies of scale. For example, the electronic massagers and medical devices produced in Xiapu and toys in Fuding have both good economic and social benefits. We must do all we can to increase their output and scale. They can only occupy a greater market share by reaching the proper scale. We can also consider establishing an industrial project database that is constantly updated. As long as there are good projects, there will be funding. Funds can be raised from multiple channels, and more joint stock enterprises can be formed.

Poverty alleviation is another important task in Ningde Prefecture. It has a large impoverished area, and after three years of poverty alleviation, there have been some heartening changes. But we should clearly see that poverty alleviation is still at a low level and still unstable. This is a long-term, arduous task, and we must make mental preparations for a protracted battle. Poverty alleviation requires a change of attitude and mentally wearing away at the "poverty mentality." We should not be constantly harping on about poverty. Some townships that are developing pretty well include themselves in the scope of impoverished regions. This can only have a negative effect. Furthermore, we must clearly lay out our poverty alleviation measures, and whether it is planting and cultivation, animal husbandry, or the processing industry, we should strive for "one product for each village" (each village should focus on a specialized product). Houyang Village in Fu'an County raised village-wide average incomes to over RMB800 per person through planting Kyoho grapes, thereby casting off the shackles of poverty. Mushrooms and tealeaves are important poverty-alleviation projects for suburban farmers, and the departments in each county must provide technical support to bring farmers from poverty to prosperity. Third, we must combine poverty alleviation with rural socialist cultural progress. Some farmers in Shouning County live alongside their livestock in squalid conditions, and the counties must help these farmers plan and build their rural residences to separate people from their livestock. The vicious cycle of "poverty-unsanitary conditions-disease-poverty" must be broken. Fourth, a portion of poverty alleviation funds must be used to support rural collective economic entities to give us the stamina needed for poverty alleviation. For households hit hard by years of disease and natural disasters, we must give them appropriate relief and help them develop production projects that they are capable of.

The She people of Ningde account for 40% of the country's She population and 70% of the province's. Most of the She people live in remote mountainous areas and are relatively impoverished. Working with ethnic minority groups is a fundamental task for us, and a basic part of our Party's ethnic policies is to strive for equality and unity for ethnic groups. Ethnic work is rooted in developing the economy, as true ethnic equality can only come with a good economy. We must formulate special preferential policies for supporting the rural development of areas inhabited by minorities and offer them better assistance. We must focus on training minority officials, developing and documenting ethnic culture, and providing good secondary education to minorities.

All of this will gradually help the "weak hatchling birds" fill out with strong wings and create the necessary conditions for being the first to "take flight."

4. Lofty ambitions

Without the lofty ambition of steadfast integrity and constantly serving the people, it is difficult to maintain long-term flight and "soar high."

Strictly governing the Party and governance with integrity are linked to the success and failure of reform and opening up, and they are continually the lifelines of the Party. We absolutely cannot allow people to seek personal gain from the power they have been given. The principal aim of being an official is to contribute and serve. "Both things you desire cannot be obtained at once."[4] Officials cannot also covet wealth – "don't extend your hand; the extended hand will be caught."[5] Of course, while advocating a clean government with integrity, we must also differentiate illegal behavior and discipline violations from mistakes made in the course of reform and opening up. It is important to keep up the enthusiasm of reformers and encourage officials to be the first to act for the people's causes. We must both dare to punish wrongdoing and be good at providing incentives, and we must always make sure we have good policies.

As for Ningde Prefecture, I am fully confident that through our tireless hard work we can create a miracle of the "weak hatchling bird" being the first to take flight in many areas.

Notes

[1] In Book 30 of *A General Source for Remarks on Poetry*, the Song Dynasty's Ruan Yue quoted a line from *Chats on Past and Contemporary Poetry*, "during the reign of the Tang Dynasty Emperor Dali, the Buddhist monk Yuan Lan inscribed this poem on a piece of bamboo, 'Fish frolic in the vast sea and birds soar in the open skies.'" This poem expressed the monk's magnanimity and animated language. It was later revised, "Fish can leap at will in a boundless sea, and birds can soar free beneath the limitless sky." It is a metaphor for the ability to move without constraints or display one's abilities freely.

[2] This expression refers to obvious matters that are right under one's nose and should have been handled with the proper attention, yet are forgotten and treated with neglect. It is based on a line from the Tang Dynasty writer Du Mu (803-853), in his poem "Climbing Chizhou's Nine-peak Tower with Zhang Hu." It reads, "They fail to see to the lashes growing before their eyes."

[3] Closing off mountains to encourage afforestation is a measure that ensures forests have the opportunity to grow. Mountainous areas that sprout young growth or have the potential to develop into forests cannot be used for pasture, timber, or

fuel during a fixed period.

[4] This expression is based on the following line from "Book 6A" of the *Mencius*, "I desire fish, and I also desire bear's paws. If I cannot have both of them, I will give up fish and take bear's paws." [Source of English translation: Mencius, "Book 6A," in *Mencius*, trans. Irene Bloom (New York: Columbia University Press, 2009), 127. – *Tr.*]

[5] This expression is from Chen Yi's poem "Seven-character Verse, Don't Extend Your Hand," in *Selected Poems of Chen Yi*. It admonishes those who harbor evil intentions, "Don't extend your hand; the extended hand will be caught. The Party and the people are watching; it is difficult to escape the public glare." A native of Lezhi, Sichuan Province, Chen Yi (1901-1972) was a Marxist, military strategist, and proletarian revolutionary. He co-founded and commanded the Chinese People's Liberation Army.

"Economic Chorus"

September 1988

Each song, each tune, has a theme. When people hear the familiar theme, they know which song or tune it is. The theme is the subject of the song, as well as its soul. There is a theme, too, in the various aspects of work in a place: socialist economic development. Once, on an inspection of a township in Ningde, I saw that the local government office's walls were hung with numerous award banners for achieving "Excellence" and being "Number One" in many areas of work. Unfortunately, however, none of them had anything to do with economic development. Here it is worth asking: Can we say that there was a theme? I think not! Hanging up so many award banners without one for economic development was not very impressive. To put it more politely, it reflected working hard without performing a true service. Working without setting priorities and sticking to the fundamentals is simply tinkering.

To sing in unison, a choir must focus on the theme and the rhythm. The same is true of economic work. If every entity only stresses the importance of its own work, each following its own score and singing a different tune, the performance will inevitably fail. So, we must advocate an "economic chorus."

Such a chorus must have a conductor. The conductor at the local level is the local Party committee and government. Modern society has entered an era of large economies and mass production. Attention must be paid to all aspects of planning, research, production, transportation, sales, and service. The failure of any aspect will result

11

in the interruption of economic activity; a weak link will become a bottleneck in development, affecting normal activity. The work of the various departments and units participating in the "chorus" is quite complex, with different instruments and voices. "The big strings plang-planged like swift-falling rain; the little strings went buzz-buzz like gentle whispers"[1]; nevertheless, they must follow the conducting of the Party and the government. We must all sing together, focusing on the theme of economic work. No matter whether the chorus is "classical" or "pop," as long as there is a theme and a rhythm, it has an artistic appeal. Otherwise, with the Party committee singing one tune, the people's congress singing another, the people's political consultative conference singing a different tune, and the government singing yet another, there can be nothing but cacophony[2], and this place will certainly not sing its song well.

An "economic chorus" requires coordination and cooperation. It will not do to have a theme only but not work together or, even worse, engage in internal friction and discord. We must mobilize enthusiasm in each department and every aspect. Since it is a chorus, all departments must consciously cooperate and take the initiative to coordinate. This is not a simple "1 + 1 = 2" formula; what we want is "1 + 1 > 2," which is often called the benefit of integration. Let's compare it to a soccer match. In high-level world soccer competition today, focusing only on personal skills and individual footwork is no longer the prevailing trend. Scoring relies mainly on the organic cooperation of the players, and coordination is now an important aspect of tactical awareness on the soccer field. A famous soccer commentator said with regard to Argentina's painful loss in the 12th World Cup final: "As a star player, Maradona focused only on the individual and not the collective. The individualistic style of the Argentine star ultimately resulted in their loss of this World Cup championship." Soccer fans often criticize some players for "dribbling too much" because they dislike it when players show off their own skills, which damages organic cooperation and misses opportunities to score. In local economic work, all departments at different levels – upper and lower, related and unrelated – must form an integrated whole. Each department has relative independence but is part of the whole, and cannot be separate from the whole or cut off relations with other departments. "To see (only) one hair of a thoroughbred horse is not to know its shape; to see (only) one color of a painting is not to know its beauty."[3] Any department acting as a "lone wolf" is working against the integrated strategy. Every official should be aware that, if you have a place in the chorus, you have a duty to cooperate.

For the economic chorus to have strong artistic value, it must adhere to choral discipline as well as to technique. Each department and every individual must therefore be conscious of the overall strategy. With the same goal, concerted efforts, and a unified voice, we will produce a melodious, resonant, and beautiful song.

Notes

[1] See Bai Juyi, "Song of the Lute." A Tang Dynasty poet, Bai Juyi (772-846) was from Taiyuan, Shanxi Province, and later moved to Xiagui (north of modern Weinan, Shaanxi Province). His most celebrated poems include "Song of Lasting Pain," "The Old Charcoal Seller," and "Song of the Lute." [Source of English translation: Bai Juyi, "Song of the Lute," in *Po Chü-i: Selected Poems*, trans. Burton Watson (New York: Columbia University Press, 2000), 79. – *Tr.*]

[2] See Qiu Chi, "Letter to Chen Bozhi." A native of Wucheng, Wuxing Prefecture (modern Huzhou, Zhejiang), Qiu Chi (464-508) was a writer from the Southern Liang Dynasty. He composed one of the finest examples of parallel prose from that time, "Letter to Chen Bozhi," in order to persuade the general Chen Bozhi to leave the state of Wei and return to the state of Liang.

[3] See Shi Jiao, the *Shizi*. A Legalist from the Warring States period, Shi Jiao (c. 390-330 BC) is believed to have been a teacher to the statesman Shang Yang. Shi Jiao advocated establishing a legal system upon which to rule the land. His book, the *Shizi*, was banned and eventually disappeared as a result of the Han Dynasty practice of "venerating only Confucian arts." People from later generations, including the Tang Dynasty's Wei Zheng and the Qing Dynasty's Zhang Zongshun, worked to reconstruct the text. [Source of English translation: Shi Jiao, "Fragments," in *Shizi: China's First Syncretist*, trans. Paul Fischer (New York: Columbia University Press, 2012), 166. – *Tr.*]

The Basic Proficiency of Officials
– Maintaining Close Ties with the People

January 1989

The unique geographical locations and specific economic development conditions of impoverished areas mean that development and change in those places can only be a gradual process. To fundamentally alter poverty and backwardness, the people there must engage in a long-term, unremitting effort with an entrepreneurial spirit of tenacity and dedication, like "water droplets drilling through rock." To this end, officials in impoverished areas have a more arduous task than others. What kind of basic proficiency, then, is required of these officials? To answer this question, we must look at the larger question of the basic conditions for development and change in poor areas. What does the development of impoverished areas rely on? Most fundamentally, there are only two things: first, the Party's leadership and, second, the power of the people. The Party's leadership is embodied in the Party's guidelines, principles, and policies, which are executed by our officials. Only when they go out among the people and maintain close ties with them can officials better implement the Party's principles and policies. This is one aspect of the answer. The other aspect is that the people need leadership. Without leadership, we can neither increase or sustain the enthusiasm of the people. In order to lead, we must have credibility; there can be no real leadership without credibility. Where does a leader's credibility come from? It does not come from relying on higher authorities, exerting power, or using gimmicks. It is only built gradually by working for the people wholeheartedly,

14

with dedication and perseverance. A leader must be proficient. Where does such proficiency come from? It comes from understanding and mastering objective laws, which is embedded in practice among the people.

To improve our proficiency as leaders, we must look to the grass-roots and absorb our nutrients from working among the people, obtaining genuine knowledge. So, whether we are developing the Party's leadership role or stimulating the enthusiasm of the people, we require our officials at all levels to maintain close ties with the people. This is a very important basic proficiency for officials, who should practice it diligently. On our way forward, there will be many problems and difficulties. Exactly where should we start to solve the problems, and on what should we rely to overcome the difficulties? We can discuss different ideas and methods from various angles. The fundamental thing, however, is to mobilize and rely on the people. This requires our leading officials at all levels to become deeply involved with the people in real situations, always coming from the people and going to the people. An official who does not understand this or does not persist in doing so accordingly will not possess such basic proficiency and is not a competent leader.

Harvard University professor John King Fairbank posed a question in his book, *The Great Chinese Revolution*: "As of 1928 China's future seemed to be with the KMT; …How come the situation was reversed twenty years later?"[1] His answer was: "the KMT leadership was older and had become worn out"[2] and "alienated…the Chinese people."[3] Meanwhile the leaders of the Communist Party of China, in Fairbank's view, "were…fervently devoted to their cause, and they pioneered…, on the cutting edge of a great national upheaval."[4] He recognized the problem of the common aspiration of the people, which is rare for a bourgeois scholar. His words certainly point to the root cause of victory in the Chinese revolution – the Party's close relationship with the people. The patriot and democracy advocate Huang Yanpei[5] said to Mao Zedong[6]: Few people, families, groups, localities, or even nations, have the capacity to break free of this cycle.

At first they carefully focus on every issue, and everyone exerts their best effort. Conditions may be quite difficult at the time, and they must struggle for their very survival. As things gradually change for the better, they gradually lose their focus. Complacency then arises, spreads from a few to the many, and becomes the norm. Even with a great effort, the situation cannot be reversed. Huang hoped that the "members of the Communist Party" would be able to find a new way forward to escape the historical cycle in which rulers in the past had moved from hard work and innovation to becoming isolated from the people. Mao Zedong immediately answered: We have found a new path and we can break this cycle. This new path is democracy, and the mass line. When the people are allowed to monitor the government, it dare not become lax. When everyone bears responsibility, the death of the ruler will not cause the government to collapse. Mao Zedong summarized the theory and practice of the Party and made the great and solemn call to "serve the people wholeheartedly,"[7] which was written into the Party Constitution as the sole purpose of our Party. We can see that maintaining close ties with the people is determined by the very nature and mission of our Party, and it is also an excellent tradition and style forged and upheld throughout its long revolutionary struggle. We must understand from this high vantage point why officials must work hard to practice the basic proficiency of maintaining close ties with the people.

Advocating close ties with the people is of even more practical significance today. Generally speaking, our Party and officials have a good relationship with the people. But in recent years we have also seen some officials engaging in bureaucratism, subjectivism, formalism, individualism, abuse of power, and other corrupt practices. In some cases these have become rather serious problems. The people have reacted strongly to it, raising strenuous objections. As early as 50 years ago, Zhou Enlai[8] warned the entire Party: Defeats in battle are less to be feared than the low morale of the people! If we lose popular support, the situation will be irretrievable.[9] If we do not focus on close ties with the people, we will lose the blood-and-flesh relationship between our Party and the people established during the difficult years of China's revolutionary war. Success in governance lies in following the hearts of the people; failure lies in opposing the hearts of the people.[10] Our Party has been in power for 40 years of peacetime. The danger of becoming isolated from the people has greatly increased compared to during wartime, and the potential harm of such isolation to the Party and the people is also much greater.

At present we are placing great emphasis on social stability. What is our most important safeguard? It is the people, the tens of millions who wholeheartedly support the Four Cardinal Principles[11] and reform and opening up. "Governance lies in reassuring the people; reassuring the people lies in observing their suffering."[12] This ancient saying about governance is still worth drawing from today. As long as we understand and address the suffering of the people, "dispelling the suffering of the people like treating your own severe illness."[13] As long as we truly represent the fundamental interests of the people and "take as our own the mind of the people,"[14] the people will gather around us, and we need not worry about social instability. As the poet Gu Yanwu[15] of the Ming Dynasty wrote, "In the mountains Goujian lived / His countrymen their lives would give."[16] He meant that Goujian, the king of Yue, lived in the Kuaiji Mountains and patiently suffered hardships to build up strength against the invading neighbor state of Wu, winning the trust of the people, who then became willing to sacrifice themselves for him. The fundamental interests of the feudal monarch were contrary to those of the people, but when he arrived among the people, showed willingness to stand up for them and desired to share their joys and sorrows to some extent, the people were ready to die for him. The fundamental interests of our Party's officials conform with those of the people. So long as we stay close to the people and truly share their pains and concerns, we will certainly reaffirm our close ties with the people and win their hearts and minds.

Party members and officials must have close ties with the people; this is not just a slogan, but should be translated into real action. In view of our actual situation, the most important things we can do now for close ties with the people are to follow the mass line, run the Party with strict discipline, and do solid work for the people.

To follow the mass line, we must first have a mass viewpoint. "What truly is within will be manifested without."[17] With a mass viewpoint, close ties with the people will become a conscious act. Second, we must frequently go in-depth to the grassroots, deep down among the people, and have more and wider channels of contacting with them. This year, we will adopt three measures in the Ningde Prefecture. The first is to have prefectural and county leaders go to the grassroots to set up an on-site office; the second is for leadership at all levels to establish a Public Reception Day system; and the third is for leading officials to establish special links with grassroots units. I believe that, through these measures, we will not only further the implementation of our plans, but also forge closer relationships between officials and the people, improve our working practices, and enhance the sense of responsibility and mission among leading officials at all levels.

Most fundamental to governing the Party with strict discipline is to gain the people's trust and support through upright practices to restore and develop the Party's fine way of conduct. It is very important for Party members and officials to be incorruptible as well as diligent. Throughout Chinese history, there have been many examples of honest and hard-working officials. The ancient statesman and strategist Zhuge Liang,[18] who strove humbly to "do his best until death,"[19] required himself "not to allow himself or his family to have extra possessions in or out of the household."[20] The Song Dynasty scholar-official Sima Guang[21] "desired to sacrifice himself for his country and attend personally to public matters, working day and night."[22] He was "indifferent to material things, with no special interest in them,"[23] and "wore coarse clothing and ate poor food until the end of his life."[24] If feudal officials were capable of this, who says that our proletarian officials are not? The older generation of proletarian revolutionaries, as represented by Chairman Mao Zedong, were models of honesty and diligence. Our officials at all levels must learn from the older generation of proletarian revolutionaries, and strive to "be incorrupt-ible and diligent without complaint of poverty or hardship."[25] In this way, we can always be rooted in the people.

To do good deeds for the people, we must be in a constant, down-to-earth way, for a better result. The people are the most realistic. They not only want to hear what you say, they also want to see how you do it. They not only want to hear your "nice singing," they also want to see your "nice performance." The impoverished region is backward with a weak economic foundation. The people there have many difficulties that need to be solved. We have no choice but to assess our strengths and do what we can, striving to do good deeds for the people. On many issues, it is impossible to do as people would expect. But as long as we do a few real things for the people each year, they will wholeheartedly support us and voluntarily work with us to tackle the difficulties together. Some colleagues say that it needs money to do things. This is not off the mark, but it does not address the whole situation. Doing real good deeds for the people is multifac-eted. At the grassroots, it is resolving practical difficulties for people in work and life. It is going to the countryside to promote the Party's rural policies, improving education, and resolving peoples' concerns. It is helping to strengthen grassroots Party building and promote rural economic development. It is also conducting surveys and case studies, and summing up the experience to guide our work.

To do real good deeds, we must focus on broadening our vision and free our minds. First, we must have a dialectical understanding of doing real good deeds; it does not simply mean handing out money and materials. We need to do real deeds for material development, but also for intellectual and cultural progress.

Second, we must know where to focus. We must focus on the people's most urgent problems in work and life. The "hot" and "diffi-cult" issues attracting the greatest public concern are where we should strive the most to resolve. We cannot evade the hard issues and focus on the easy ones, concentrate on trivial matters while neglecting important ones, or avoid tough problems.

Third, we must improve our proficiency in doing real good deeds, focus on doing practical things rationally, and promote scientific thinking and reasoning in the process. In assessing whether we are doing something meaningful and valuable, we must consider not only the immediate needs of the people, but also whether there will be unintended consequences, whether it will "solve one problem, but leave ten regrets." For example, if we build a dike, the problem of pedestrian and car traffic will be solved, but, if there is no water flow, we have destroyed the ecological balance. If we extensively use geothermal water, the people will be able to take therapeutic baths more easily and be happy, but structures on the ground surface may sink, bringing about more intractable problems. We should never do such stupid things! "Not expending useless effort or engaging in meaningless activity"[26] should be our motto for doing real deeds for the people.

Fourth, we must have a holistic view, uphold Party principles, and do things in accordance with policies. We must not take on projects that are only partially but not fully feasible. We cannot act for the short term, especially in pursuit of our own personal achievements with reckless disregard for policies and regulations. In doing real deeds, we must make it a process of educating the people about patriotism, socialism, collectivism, and the Party's principles and policies. In this way, people will personally experience the attention of the Party and the government, as well as the superiority of the socialist system, so that they support the Party and socialism wholeheartedly even more.

Notes

[1] John K. Fairbank, *The Great Chinese Revolution, 1800-1985* (New York: Harper & Row, 1986), 218.

[2] *Ibid.*

[3] *Ibid.*, 263.

[4] *Ibid.*, 210.

[5] A native of Chuansha (now part of Shanghai's Pudong New Area), Jiangsu Province, Huang Yanpei (1878-1965) was an educator and democratic revolutionary.

[6] A native of Xiangtan, Hunan Province, Mao Zedong (1893-1976) was a Marxist, Chinese proletarian revolutionary, strategist, and theorist. He was one of the principal founders of the Communist Party of China, the Chinese People's Liberation Army, and the People's Republic of China. He was the leader of all ethnic groups in China and the principal founder of Mao Zedong Thought.

[7] Source of English translation: Mao Zedong, *Quotations from Chairman Mao Tse-Tung* (Beijing: Foreign Language Press, 1966), 170. – *Tr.*

[8] Zhou Enlai (1898-1976) was born in Huai'an, Jiangsu Province. His ancestral home was Shaoxing, Zhejiang Province. He was a Marxist, Chinese proletarian revolutionary, statesman, military strategist, and diplomat. He was one of the principal leaders of the Communist Party of China, the People's Republic of China, and the Chinese People's Liberation Army, which he co-founded.

[9] Source of English translation: Zhou Enlai, "The Present Crisis in the War of Resistance and the Tasks To Be Undertaken in Pursuing the War in North China," in *Selected Works of Zhou Enlai* (Beijing: Foreign Language Press, 1981), 101. – *Tr.*

[10] Source of English translation: Guan Zi, "Mu Min" ("On Shepherding the People"), in *Guanzi: Political, Economic, and Philosophical Essays from Early China, A Study and Translation,* trans. W. A. Rickett (Boston: Cheng & Tsui, 2001), 54. – *Tr.*

[11] The Four Cardinal Principles are to adhere to the socialist path, adhere to the people's democratic dictatorship, adhere to the leadership of the Communist Party of China, and adhere to Marxism-Leninism and Mao Zedong Thought. These principles are the foundation of the state, and the political cornerstone for the survival and development of the Party and the nation.

[12] This is based on a line in Zhang Juzheng's "Memorial to the Emperor Proposing Taxes Be Waived to Reassure the People." It reads, "The primary task of government is to reassure the people; the Way to reassure the people is to understand their suffering." A native of Jiangling in Huguang Province (modern Jingzhou, Hubei Province), Zhang Juzheng (1525-1582) was a Ming Dynasty statesman.

[13] See Su Zhe, "Letter to the Emperor." A native of Meishan, Meizhou (now in

Sichuan Province), Su Zhe (1039-1112) was a prose writer from the Northern Song Dynasty. He is remembered as one of the "Eight Prose Masters of the Tang and Song."

[14] See chapter 49 of *Dao De Jing*. A thinker from the Spring and Autumn Period (770-476 BC), Lao Zi was the founder of Daoism. He is believed to have come from Ku County in the state of Chu (east of modern Luyi, Henan Province, or Woyang, Anhui Province). He proposed "the Way [models itself] on that which is naturally so," "Something and Nothing produce each other," "govern by doing nothing," and many other simple examples of dialectical thinking. [D.C. Lau, p. 82, 58] He is the reputed author of *Dao De Jing (also translated as Tao Te Ching)*, which is also known as *Laozi* and *Five-Thousand-Character Text by Lao Zi*. [Source of English translation: Lao Zi, *Tao Te Ching*, trans. D.C. Lau (Harmondsworth: Penguin Books Ltd., 1972), 110. – *Tr.*]

[15] A native of Kunshan, Jiangsu Province, Gu Yanwu (1613-1682) was a thinker, Confucian scholar, historian, geographer, and phonologist. Together with Huang Zongxi and Wang Fuzhi, he is considered one of the three greatest Confucian scholars from the late Ming (1368-1644) and early Qing (1644-1911) dynasties. He developed a new method of scholarly research and was venerated for carrying on the heritage and paving the way for future generations. Honored with the title "founding father of simple and plain learning," he spent his later years studying the classics and developing the field of textual criticism.

[16] See Gu Yanwu's poem "Autumn Hills."

[17] See *The Great Learning*. Part of the Confucian canon, *The Great Learning* expounds on the relationship between the self-cultivation of individuals and the stability of society. Originally included in *The Book of Rites*, it was extracted during the Song Dynasty (960-1279) as a standalone book. Along with *The Doctrine of the Mean*, *The Analects*, and *Mencius*, it is considered one of the "Four Books." [Source of English translation: Zeng Zi, "The Great Learning," in *The Four Books*, trans. James Legge (New York: Paragon Book Reprint Corp., 1966), 324. (Reprinted from *The Four Books*, Shanghai 1923 edition). – *Tr.*]

[18] A native of Yangdu, Langya (south of modern Yinan, Shandong Province), Zhuge Liang (181-234) was a statesman and military strategist in the state of Shu Han during the Three Kingdoms Period (220-280). Later generations honored him with the title "Martial Marquis Zhuge." With the determination to perform his duties until his last breath, he personifies loyalty and wisdom in traditional Chinese culture.

[19] See Zhuge Liang, "Later Memorial to Launch a Campaign."

[20] See Zhuge Liang, "Memorial to Emperor Liu Shan."

[21] Sima Guang (1019-1086) was a minister and historian in the Northern Song Dynasty (960-1127). He was from Sushui Township, Xia County, Shaanxi Province

(now in Shanxi Province). He compiled the *Comprehensive Mirror for the Aid of Government*, which was the first general history of ancient China to be organized as a chronicle. It documented 1,362 years of history, beginning with the 23rd year of King Weilie of Zhou's reign (403 BC) and ending with the reign of Emperor Shizong of Later Zhou (959).

[22] See "Biography of Sima Guang," in *History of the Song*. The *History of the Song* was compiled by the Yuan Dynasty's Tuo Tuo et al. It recorded the history of the Song Dynasty in the form of biographies, and is considered an essential reference for any study of the Song Dynasty.

[23] See "Biography of Sima Guang," in *History of the Song*.

[24] *Ibid.*

[25] This is an old adage that was written in the form of a couplet and displayed in an accounting room at the offices of the Neixiang County Government in Henan Province. The first line reads, "Be incorruptible and diligent without complaint of poverty or hardship." The second line reads, "Value sound advice and implement sensible ideas."

[26] See the chapter "On Maintaining Restraint," in *Guanzi*. Compiled by the Western Han Dynasty's Liu Xiang, parts of *Guanzi* was written by scholars from the Jixia Academy under the name of Guan Zhong during the Warring States Period (475-221 BC). A native of Pei (modern Pei County, Jiangsu Province), Liu Xiang (c. 77-6 BC) was a Confucian scholar, bibliographer, and writer from the Western Han Dynasty. Guan Zhong (?-645 BC) was from Yingshang. He was a statesman for the state of Qi during the early Spring and Autumn Period. [Source of English translation: Guan Zi, "Jin Cang (On Maintaining Restraint)," in *Guanzi: Political, Economic, and Philosophical Essays from Early China, A Study and Translation,* vol. 2, trans. W. A. Rickett (Princeton: Princeton University Press, 1998), 219. – *Tr.*]

The Glories of Ningde
– Thoughts on Cultural Progress

January 1990

People do not do well without pressure. Wang Jinxi[1] once said that a well without pressure produces no oil, and people without pressure tend to be lightweights. We recognize that Ningde is poor, and clearly see that the road ahead will have many twists and turns. Poverty gives rise to the desire for change, and we can move forward in the face of adversity. The pressure of such "poverty" therefore has its benefits. Yet pressure alone does not work. If people see only the poverty without a historical perspective, a development outlook, it is easy to lose self-confidence and self-esteem. It is also easy to let outsiders have a peculiar "pity and commiseration," which can be expressed as sympathy, but also as withdrawal and disdain. Such pressure is negative. So, when we discuss poverty, we should not forget to consider the glories of Ningde. When we mention pressure, let us not forget to discuss motivation.

What is glorious about Ningde? I think that its beautiful rivers and mountains are a kind of glory. The area's splendid cultural traditions are also glorious. Another glory is its people's spirit of self-reliance, hard work, kindness, honesty, and simplicity. Only when conscious of our own glory can we have self-confidence, self-esteem, and the vigorous impetus to forge ahead. There is a proverb that says, "Granny Wang boasts about her melons for sale," which is flavored with irony. Yet if the melons are really good and have their own special features, why not boast about them? This is also a manifestation of self-esteem and self-confidence. There is no harm in our being like Granny Wang,

24

which is not easy. We must fully understand our wares to describe them well and make people interested.

The people of Ningde must first have a good understanding of our own land. If we do not, how can we come to love Ningde, much less develop it? We can help people understand the glories of Ningde from the perspective of cultural progress. The people of Ningde have a need for self-awareness; just being born and growing up in this place does not mean one knows it well. Some people are not very familiar with Ningde, do not understand it, and are unaware of the wonderful history of their homeland. Or, even if they do know it, they do not understand why it is the way it is, so they simply envy others and lose self-confidence. This lack of awareness is well described in a line from a poem: "Why can't I tell the true shape of Mount Lushan? / Because I myself am in the mountain."[2] From this perspective, cultural progress means improving people's ethical and cultural lives. If the people in a place are depressed and pessimistic, we cannot say that good cultural progress has been made there. Also, as we engage in reform and opening up, we should allow more outsiders to gain a fuller understanding of Ningde. This is important because we want to show off the area to increase its attractiveness. If a place does not have much appeal to outsiders, we cannot say that reform and opening up have gone well there. This also shows that cultural progress is closely linked to reform and opening up.

There are many things involved in a region's cultural progress. An important aspect is to carry forward the traditional culture of that place. Throughout the entire country, China's traditional culture has played a positive role in the continuity and development of the nation. In the history of civilization over thousands of years, we have established a strong sense of national self-confidence. In times of both peril and prosperity, such self-confidence is the most stable ingredient of our national spirit. It is this self-confidence that has allowed the Chinese people to make it through many internal and external crises in modern history, and has brought the Chinese nation to its admirable position in the world today. Cultural progress in Ningde has the same significance. We have a clear goal: promote the nation's fine traditions through cultural undertakings to enhance our own self-confidence, and at the same time increase the confidence of the outside world in Ningde.

Such a goal requires us to have good grasp of what is glorious about Ningde. For example, it is enriched by the culture of the region's She ethnic group. Ningde is also a region with a long period of revolutionary struggle, and its people are now seizing the opportunity to become prosperous. In addition, the region is graced by a unique landscape, where the mountains meet the sea.

Cultural progress requires public awareness. In discussing public awareness, there is the question of effectiveness, which involves both content and form of the message. Content is the soul and starting point of the message, but we cannot simply yell and scream about the glories of Ningde. In any culture-building activity, we should pay attention to the format of the activity and how the methods are used. If the format and methods are not acceptable to the audience, the content cannot be delivered, and the public awareness activity will have no effect. The old saying has it right: "Words without elegance will not become popular."[3]

Which formats are good? We can continue to explore this point, but should at least focus on the following: First, it must be something the people love to see and hear that also has content, not just form for form's sake. Second, it should have public appeal. Something isolated from the people will not win their enthusiasm. Third, we can spend less while doing more, focusing on cost-effectiveness. Even a few coins thrown into the water make some sound and have an impact. Fourth, we should conform to people's tastes and not be too highbrow.

In all aspects of cultural progress in Ningde, we can do a few representative, practical things because the time is right. I suggest that we first hold a She Culture Festival. We have learned a great deal about the She ethnic culture, including new songs, folklore, proverbs, folk music and dance, folk tales, arts and crafts, heritage, and martial arts. The conditions are in place to organize a festival to exhibit the She culture. Second, I have long had the idea of making a

TV program, using the modern communication tool of television to display the glorious aspects of Ningde. We can bring together beautiful images and songs, integrating audio-visuals and scenes to present the flavor of Ningde with a broad appeal. We can envision combining the native and the "foreign." I have developed a program with experts from the provincial musicians association for making a TV documentary called "Symphony of Mountains and Seas." In the Ningde region we already have lyricists and musicians who can play their role, and we can invite singers from other places. Such creative formats can make people better acquainted with Ningde. We should have the confidence to make a television documentary to show to the whole nation.

If we fully understand and broadcast the glorious aspects of Ningde, more people – from other regions, provinces, and countries – will learn about what Ningde has to offer. In this way everyone will want to be part of Ningde, love it, and pour their heart and soul into it.

Notes

[1] A native of Yumen, Gansu Province, Wang Jinxi (1923-1970) was called "Iron Man" for his work in the oil fields. He is celebrated as a champion of the working class and was a model member of the Communist Party of China. He is considered a hero to the Chinese people for his part in developing the nation's oil industry and building socialism. In addition to the material wealth his work brought the nation, he left behind great spiritual wealth in the form of his dedication – the "Iron Man" spirit.

[2] See Su Shi (1037-1101), "Written on the Wall at West Forest Temple." [Source of English translation: Su Shi, "Written on the Wall at West Forest Temple," in *Selected Poems of Su Tung-p'o,* trans. Burton Watson (Port Townsend: Copper Canyon Press, 1994), 108. – Tr.]

[3] See "The Twentieth Year of Duke Xiang of Lu," in *Zuo's Chronicles.* Generally attributed to Zuo Qiuming, *Zuo's Chronicles,* also called *Zuo's Commentary on the Spring and Autumn Annals,* is considered part of the Confucian canon. Along with *Gongyang's* and *Guliang's,* it is one of the "Three Commentaries" that explain the *Spring and Autumn Annals.*

Clean Government Is the Historical Mission of Communists

February 1990

China has an old teaching: "The one who wins the heart of the people wins an empire."[1] What, then, do we Chinese Communists do to win the heart of the people? We rely on integrity and serving the people wholeheartedly. This is a truism. The New Democratic Revolution and socialist development have proven it. The political turmoil of 1989[2] also taught us from the negative side: Clean government is the historical mission of us Communists. If we do not take up this mission, we will lose the heart of the people and offer vulnerabilities to our enemies.

It should be noted that, on the whole, our Party has withstood the double test of being the ruling party and engaging in reform and opening up. The majority of Party members are dedicated to serving the public. We have reached a point, though, where the corruption of a small number of people within the Party has reached an intolerable point. We must punish them to assuage the people's anger. At one time the "inevitability of corruption" was a popular idea; some believe that reform and opening up is bound to give rise to corruption. If that is true, then reform and opening up has not inspired the people, but has made them decadent; it has not strengthened Party cohesion, but has demoralized it – this is certainly not the reform and opening up that we want. The nature of our Party's mission and of the social-ist system mean that we cannot tolerate corruption to creep up and spread. Our goal is not only to develop the economy, but also to have a clean and orderly government!

Coming into contact with the realities of Ningde, its impoverished areas and lack of basic resources, we realize that the task of overcoming poverty is quite difficult. It demands even more that we address clean government in order to unite and lead the people. But some people use power to make money, engage in graft and take bribes, and use unpaid labor to create their own personal world of pleasure. Some, when they lack building materials[3], misappropriate public supplies, even those to be used in education, poverty alleviation, or disaster relief. Yet others are as daring as vice-chairman Zheng of our regional Federation of Overseas Chinese who went so far as to pocket donations from overseas Chinese for personal use. If we are not "the first to worry about the affairs of the state and the last to enjoy oneself," and act like these people instead, then what hope does our cause have, and why should the 2.7 million people of Ningde trust us?

We therefore have no choice but to fight corruption and emphasize clean government. In late 1988, as we studied the overall work plan for our prefecture in 1989, we decided to strengthen Party building, crack down on corruption, and promote the reform and opening up. Then, at the prefectural Party committee's working meeting in January 1989, we decided to highlight the three areas in our fight against corruption: officials misappropriating land to put up buildings in violation of law and Party discipline, abusing their power in project contracting, and engaging in graft and taking bribes. To begin our full deployment of the fight against corruption, we decided to severely punish officials who misappropriated land for building housing for themselves.

Over the past year, through the joint efforts of the entire region, we have seen significant results in punishing corruption and building a clean government. We have essentially put an end to officials misappropriating land for building housing for themselves in violation of law and discipline, abusing their power in project contracting, and other unhealthy trends. We have made significant progress on investigations of major graft and bribery cases, a sign of the resolute determination of the prefectural and county Party committees to punish corruption and engage in clean government. The problem we face now is how to consolidate these victories, close in on the cornered adversary, and take the fight against corruption even further.

We Communists must make our historical mission of building a clean government a long-term task. We must successfully cross two hurdles. The first hurdle is within ourselves. V. I. Lenin said that people of political nobility will not become corrupt. The poor character and tainted thoughts of our officials is not only an important cause for corruption, it is also an obstacle to punishing corruption. Without rectifying ourselves, how can we rectify others? "To bring peace to the world, one must first rectify oneself."[4] We must therefore continually strengthen our self-discipline for clean government and honest public service, which is inseparable from our conscious acceptance of education. We must receive an education in basic Marxist theory, socialism, and patriotism, the revolutionary tradition, hard work and struggle, and our national conditions. The second hurdle is relationship-ism. Fighting corruption is bound to involve specific people. If it involves our friends, former schoolmates, or relatives, will we be upright, plain-spoken, impartial, and incorruptible? Or, will we be lenient, trivialize large matters, and make small ones go away? If so, if we abandon our principles for one person, we will lose the trust of tens of millions of people!

It is not a question of whether to cross these two hurdles; we simply must do it. Of course, surpassing the two hurdles merely lays a foundation. We must also begin to fundamentally eradicate the breeding grounds upon which corruption depends for its survival. What are those breeding grounds? One is the abuse of power. No matter how great or small the power of us Party members, it is given to us by the people. We can only follow the will of the people and work for their interests. When the people hand over power to us, we must allow them to feel at ease when we use such power. How do we make the people feel at ease? A very important way is to establish regulations and rules. Establishing a complete, systemic, and comprehensive system to control and supervise the use of power is a fundamental means of preventing corruption. We have already implemented the "two opens and one supervision"[5] system, which we must continue to uphold and improve. This work cannot languish within the higher-level agencies; it must go down to the grassroots level. Since all of our work is to serve the people, we should and can widely accept the criticism and supervision of the people. If we have the courage to openly accept such criticism and supervision, it is an expression of our strength as Communists, and also a concrete manifestation of practicing what we preach.

Communists are confident in assuming the historical mission of building a clean government, and this confidence is based on submitting to the truth and striving for the truth in every practical action. To build a clean government in Ningde at this time, we must do three things. The first is to continue to investigate and deal with major corruption cases, expand the depth and breadth of the investigations, and conclude and publicize a few representative cases. We must quickly investigate and reach a conclusion on existing cases to let people know the outcome as soon as possible. We should follow existing leads, continue with in-depth investigations, and get to the bottom of the cases. We must also focus on finding new leads and thoroughly investigating them. In investigating and handling major cases, we must adhere to the facts, use the law as our yardstick, and arrive at conclusions that can withstand the test of history. The second is to "grasp the key aspects and stead-fastly pursue them." As we continue to investigate and deal with graft and bribery, abusing power in project contracting, and misappropriating land for building private housing, we must also address the problems of banqueting, entertaining guests, gifting, gambling, and arrears on and illegal possession of public funds. We should grasp the key aspects in several stages, analyze the causes and clarify the situation, and take effective measures to stop the trends. This will show the people that our efforts are genuine, that we dare to tackle tough problems, and that we truly intend to punish corruption. The third is to establish a clean government accountability system. If our leaders at all levels are clean and honest, being upright themselves before rectifying others, they will provide a good example from the beginning. We must strictly require our own relatives, children, and staff to refrain from sheltering, hiding, and interceding on all issues related to family and friends; to follow the Party's code of conduct; and to strictly enforce existing provisions for honesty and integrity.

In building a clean government, we must also be worthy of the honorable name of Communists!

Notes

[1] This expression is based on the following line from "Book 4A" of the *Mencius*, "There is a way to get the kingdom: get the people, and the kingdom is got. There is a way to get the people: get their hearts, and the people are got. There is a way to get their hearts: it is simply to collect for them what they like, and not to lay on them what they dislike." [Mencius, "Book 4A," in *The Works of Mencius*, trans. James Legge (New York: Dover Publications, Inc., 2013), 300. – *Tr.*] Part of the Confucian canon, the *Mencius* is a compilation of anecdotes and open discussions between Mencius and his disciples during the Warring States Period. Together with *The Great Learning*, *The Doctrine of the Mean*, and *The Analects*, it is considered one of the "Four Books."

[2] This refers to the political turmoil that took place in Beijing during the end of spring and the beginning of summer of 1989.

[3] This refers to steel, timber, and cement.

[4] See Wu Jing, "The Way of the Sovereign," in *Essentials of Government of the Zhenguan Reign*. A native of Junyi, Bianzhou (modern Kaifeng, Henan Province), the Tang Dynasty's Wu Jing (c. 670-749) was an historian who was known for his courage to speak bluntly before the emperor.

[5] "Four discussions, two opens, and one supervision" is an administrative practice in villages. Under the leadership of the village Party organization, this practice must be followed when formulating and implementing policies on important matters. According to the "four discussions," Party organizations propose; village and Party committees confer; Party meetings deliberate; and village representative assemblies and village assemblies decide. According to the "two opens," resolutions are made in the open, and the results of their implementation are made public. According to "one supervision," the process of formulating and implementing resolutions on important matters at the village level is supervised from start to finish.

A Chat About Entering Public Service

March 1990

The Fujian Provincial Institute for Leadership Science invited me here to discuss ways that young officials can develop into good leaders. Without any specialized study in this area, I can only talk about my own experience as a government official and the lessons I have learned. If I had to pick a title for this discussion, it would be "A Chat About Entering Public Service."

"Lowest-grade officials" bear heavy responsibilities

"The lowest-grade official" was an expression used to refer to a lowly county magistrate with little power in ancient China. As a former county Party secretary, I can attest that it is not easy at all to effectively lead a county. Speaking with colleagues, I have found that we share the same sentiment: While the office may be small, the responsibilities are not.

We can compare the nation to a net. More than 3,000 counties span the nation. They are the "knots" holding this net together. When these "knots" become loose, the national political scene experiences unrest. When they remain tight, the political situation is stable. Since the specifics of government decrees are ultimately implemented through the county, the quality of work being carried out at the county level affects the prosperity and security of the nation.

We can think of a county as a microcosm of society. Just as a sparrow is small but contains all the vital organs, a county has parallel

departments and organizations that roughly correspond to those of
the central government. Work at the county level is all encompassing.
It includes everything from political, economic, and cultural issues,
to the basic needs of the people at every stage of life. Some say
that diplomacy is the only work not being done at the county level.
Nevertheless, there are occasions when counties host foreign visitors.
County leaders need to know about diplomacy so they can be ready
to host the scores of foreign guests that are expected to visit as China
continues to open up. A small county may be home to hundreds of
thousands of residents, and a large one may be home to a million. The
impact of policy decisions is no trivial matter. There is no room for
carelessness. In *Ling Zhen (A Decree of Admonishment)*, Hai Rui[1] wrote,
"The most challenging post for an official is that of the county magistrate." Indeed, only those who are highly capable and broadly knowledgeable are competent enough to head a county.

There is an old saying, "The prime minister has come up from the
post of city or prefectural mayor."[2] Many of those who hold high-ranking leadership positions in the Party and the government have extensive
experience doing grassroots work. The county serves as an ideal class-
room for training officials and foster their character. Leaders currently
working at the county level should value the opportunity to study hard
and immerse themselves in their work. They should take advantage of
the chance to hone their proficiency and gain experience.

Four pitfalls for young leaders

Young leaders are the hope of the Party. In the prime of life, they
are full of enthusiasm and eager to try new ideas, yet they are not
without shortcomings. As they mature, young leaders should nurture
their strengths, downplay their weaknesses, and be wary of four
potential pitfalls.

The first pitfall is to be impatient for success. When young leaders
assume a new position, they have a tendency to hack away at problems
to get results. This ambition and drive for recognition is commend-

able. Without a clear understanding of the situation, however, being overeager to get results may lead to rash actions that are neither rational nor realistic. "Untangling a messy knot takes patience."[3] Those who are impatient for success run a higher risk of failure.

We often say that newly-appointed officials "set three fires" – in other words, they seek dramatic changes or showy policies. However, we must ask whether these "fires" should be set, and when it is an appropriate time to set them. Any changes or policies should be based on reality. Officials need to spend more time with the people, conduct more investigations, and clarify all the nuts and bolts. After taking stock of the situation, officials should set only necessary "fires." They must fight the urge to "set fires" just because everyone else does, after all "recklessness undermines dependability."[4] Of course, when troubles flare up, superiors may ask you to take swift and decisive action to ensure that everything runs smoothly. In these situations, it may be desirable to set "three fires." However, you still want to make sure that you understand the situation before taking action.

When your superiors assign you to work in an area for several years, they are not counting on your ability to "set three fires," but rather your tenacity to "climb mountains." Instead of trying to make breakthroughs that are dependent on "qualitative change," I believe young officials should focus on the steady, systematic work necessary for "quantitative change." I admire those who tackle problems with persistence and work with quiet dedication, like water droplets drilling through rock. I encourage officials to immerse themselves in their work and engage in long-term projects that pave the way for others. Development and change are a gradual process. Thus, qualitative change is built on an accumulation of quantitative changes. For example, history has shaped Ningde into an underdeveloped area. Quick fixes cannot change Ningde, but tenacity can. After all, streams have their beginnings in tiny droplets, and hills start out as grains of sand. An official post can never develop into a rewarding career without the will to persevere, the drive to work harder than anyone else does, and the determination to accumulate every "droplet."

The second pitfall is to be too opinionated. Most young officials have attended high school or college. While they may have gained considerable knowledge from books, they are still inexperienced and untested. As such, they are prone to the misconception that they alone are "awake" as the rest of the world sleeps[5], and tend to underestimate the importance of historical experience. A formal education is based on knowledge gleaned from the accumulated experience of myriads of working people. To look down on historical experience is to look down on the people. Nothing can be accomplished by separating oneself from the people or isolating oneself.

From the perspective of development, human knowledge is replenished on a continual basis. No one person, not even a highly intelligent person, can possibly get to the "truth" of things in just one try. All one person can get to is the "truth" at a specific stage of development. We can only approach the truth; we can never get to the bottom of it. At best, we use a lens based on the "truth" at a specific stage of development to deal with matters that have evolved over the course of countless series of events. In the theory of knowledge, this leads to metaphysical errors. In practice, it leads to dogmatic errors.

Whether tackling an issue from the perspective of practice or development, young officials must refrain from being too opinionated. Instead, try to keep an open mind, and learn from the people and more experienced officials. Try to improve through the dialectical materialism of Marxism, and then apply Marxist views and methods to observe and handle any issues. Having an overinflated sense of self encourages the rejection of the truth, which blocks young leaders from gaining insight and sabotages the chance for success.

The third pitfall is to make unpredictable changes in policy. After assuming a post, young officials will eventually hear comments about their job performance, regardless of the quality of their work. Some people will offer praise and approval, while others will voice doubts and objections. This is especially true when dealing with hot spots of society that catch the attention of the people or pressing issues that must be handled by the officials personally. The way an official deals with these issues becomes an endless source of debate. A lack of political experience predisposes young officials to believing rumors about their performance. Heaps of praise shore up their convictions. Volleys of criticism chip away at their confidence, and may even cause them to have misgivings about their handling of certain issues. These feelings are heightened when debates involve respected local figures, officials from powerful departments, and distinguished scholars. Pressure from old schoolmates, former colleagues, and fellow comrades-in-arms can be difficult to ignore. Moreover, when people from their hometowns or mentors offer their opinions, some young officials are flummoxed and fail to assert their own views. It is no wonder that some young leaders change their positions on issues as often as they brush their teeth. By making these unpredictable changes in policy, young officials become their own worst enemies.

I believe that "careful planning reduces the likelihood of bewilderment later." Before deciding on a policy, young officials should do their research, solicit a wide range of opinions, and get a firm grasp on the nature of all the issues involved. Then, consider any rules that apply, devise a plan, and make a judgment. After coming to a decision, young officials should avoid making any significant changes until after the solution has been implemented. "Brave important events without trepidation."[6] "Maintain your composure when confronted with crises that threaten your vital interests."[7] When debates flare up, refrain from the temptation to change course. When setbacks occur, refuse to allow bepuzzlement to take hold. Avoid chasing fads at all costs. In time, more people will recognize your staunch convictions and sound decisions. Debates will quiet down as problems are resolved. This is a gradual process that also helps you win the recognition you deserve.

The fourth pitfall is to have more ambition than ability. Young officials with a good education but little practical experience tend to fall into a trap: they are not competent enough to work on major projects, yet they are unwilling to handle minor assignments. In the end, they are nothing more than the Krikun[8] style. Sun Yat-sen[9] said it well, rather than setting your sights on achieving a high rank, set your resolve to achieving great things. However, great things don't just materialize out of thin air. They are achieved by accumulating small successes, because "big things must have their beginnings in the small."[10] Young officials need to be honest. They must be willing to do the most ordinary things, fill in the smallest gaps, and play the most insignificant roles. This is the way to gradually gain experience, win social recognition, and achieve extraordinary success while doing ordinary tasks.

Four essentials to being an official

All things have certain essentials that make up their basic nature. This includes officials, who manage social affairs as a profession. Since ancient times, people have attached great importance to the essentials of being an official, or the Way of an official. During the Warring States period (475-221 BC), Xun Zi[11] pointed out that while rulers hold great power, power alone cannot make the world a peaceful place. He said, "What brings peace and security will inevitably be his use of the Way."[12] In studying the Way of an official, I have learned that leading Party officials must grasp the following four points.

First, officials must have the right foundation. They must leave a positive impact with each term in office. This is in line with the purpose of our Party: to serve the people. An extreme view has gained traction in our society that those who are noble and upright are above entering public service or associating with officials. Some people believe that government is a dirty place, run by people with unclean hands. In my opinion, an "official" is simply a profession, just like a doctor or sanitation worker. Society needs people to enter different lines of work. Viewed solely as a profession, there is nothing good or bad about being an "official." However, there are good and bad officials.

Beginning with the first day on the job, officials should ask themselves two questions: Why do I want to be an official? What kind of official do I want to be? After being in politics for decades, some people become trapped by fame and fortune, some accomplish nothing at all, and still others fall from grace with a ruined reputation. These are examples of people who became officials for the wrong reasons. Before the founding of New China in 1949, people would study for many years, braving untold hardships, just so they could enter politics to honor their ancestors or put their name in the history books. Some people engaged in intrigue. They cruelly oppressed the people in order to make their fortunes by dubious means. The history of Chinese civilization is full of emperors, generals, and ministers, yet we really only remember a hundred or so of them. Li Bai[13] and Du Fu[14] were middle-ranking officials. Li Bing[15] and his son built the Dujiangyan Irrigation System, and Li Chun[16] designed the Zhaozhou Bridge, yet they weren't high-ranking officials, either. For others such as Lu Ban[17] and Huang Daopo[18], becoming an official was not even an option. Clearly, having a place in history is related to what a person does, not what rank that person holds. When the goal of becoming an official is to reap personal gain, people form cliques to pursue selfish political interests, and violate their morals to perpetrate evil schemes. In the end, the chances of surviving with their wealth or honor intact are slim to none.

An official, especially a Party official, has only one purpose: to benefit the people. This is the essential difference between an official from the Chinese Communist Party and an official from the pre-1949 government. Benefitting the people requires that officials are selfless. Only then can we eliminate corruption, which in turn provides the conditions for fair government, which then opens up opportunities to help the people find peace and contentment in their lives. Benefitting the people also requires that officials understand what the people want. This involves improving the leadership's way of work, wholly engaging with the grassroots, and developing closer ties between the Party and the people. Only then will we be on the same page as the people, eager to meet their needs, and actively working to eradicate their worries and overcome their hardships in a timely manner. Most importantly, benefitting the people requires that officials are public servants who solve real problems for the people.

Second, officials must have the right principles. To be an official requires dedication. Party officials who want to benefit the people must first be dedicated to the people. The nature and purpose of the Party have determined that they are "the first to worry about the affairs of the state and the last to enjoy oneself." Mao Zedong said, "The Communist Party is a political party that works for the interests of the nation and the people. The Party definitely does not pursue interests of its own."[19] Those who become officials in the hopes of getting rich walk a very dangerous line. Those who become officials and use their power for personal gain risk a life filled with sorrow. Chen Yi[20] warned long ago, "Don't extend your hand; the extended hand will be caught." Party discipline and national law will not tolerate any attempts by officials to use their positions in the Communist Party to amass wealth.

Centuries ago it was said, "Happy is he who is withdrawn from office." Indeed, those who become officials with the intention of living a carefree and easy life are sure to be disappointed. Being an official means taking on responsibilities. People will seek them out to complete unfinished assignments, sort out difficulties, and handle mishaps. The public will curse officials when they have grievances and need to vent. I believe that to seriously become a good Party official is hard work. I have yet to hear a leader worth his salt say that being an official is a cushy job. So, why do people still want to serve as officials? On a social level, an official is simply a profession. Someone has to do it. On a personal level, being an official means that one is to conform to the Party's cause. Those who eschew personal gain and a carefree life for the opportunity to contribute to society and the greater good, those who strive for Communist ideals, and those who assume leadership positions despite the hardships and fatigue, will live valuable lives that give them endless joy.

Third, officials must have the right morals. To be an official requires integrity. At a minimum, officials should be able to end their careers with their reputations intact. The standard for determining whether officials have conducted themselves properly must be integrity. Whether it be money or position, "if a thing doesn't belong to us, we don't dare take a hair of it."[21] Since officials hold a certain amount of power in their hands, they are at increased risk of committing mistakes when lured by money or fame. Their downfall is assured when they fail to exercise caution in their private life, do not remain vigilant against unlawful offers, or take chances engaging in illegal activities with the hope that they will not be caught. Being a leader requires using one's own moral example to win a popular following. In *The Origin of the Family, Private Property and the State,* Friedrich Engels analyzed the authority of chiefs within the clans of primitive societies. He noted, "The authority of the sachem within the gens was paternal and purely moral in character."[22] They had to "rely on the force of example."[23] Leaders wield great influence through their moral example, which is something that modern officials would do well to understand. If leading Party officials fail to become good role models by working hard despite difficulties and remaining honest as they perform their duties, then they will fail to establish trust with the people.

Fourth, officials must have the right sense of justice. To be an official requires strictly enforcing the law. This is not some personal sense of rough and tumble justice, but a commitment to promoting justice by remaining impartial and upholding morality. When the law is not strictly enforced, institutions cannot be rectified. Without strong institutions, justice cannot be upheld and morality cannot be promoted. The Northern Song Dynasty's Bao Zheng[24] believed, "When decrees are carried out, order will follow, and then there will be no poorly-governed nations or unenlightened people."[25] Some leading officials compromise their principles in order to maintain good relations. The very nature of this behavior is antithetical to the sense of justice that an official must have. Without the right sense of justice, the law becomes obscured and institutions become lax and powerless. The reason officials lack the right sense of justice is that they do not heed their own sense of decency. Officials must remember, "Do not ignore your conscience." When one listens to one's conscience, "there is no need to look outside oneself for answers." Strict and impartial laws combined with strong institutions pave the way for a secure and prosperous future. The facts show that wherever leaders remain impartial while conducting their work, remain steadfast against pressure from influential figures, and remain strict about enforcing the law, healthy tendencies increase and doing things become easier.

The importance of selecting the right people

Recognizing talent and using that talent wisely is a challenge that all leaders face. V. I. Lenin said, "Study people, search for *able* workers. This is now the essence; all orders and decisions without this are dirty bits of paper."[26] While I was working in Zhengding County, Hebei Province, the county Party committee suggested a strategy for the county: just as Fujian takes advantage of its "mountains and seas," and Qinghai develops its "grasslands and forests," Zhengding County should focus on "talent." A strategy focusing on talent can be summarized with five words: identify, choose, judge, respect, and nurture.

Leaders need to be able to define and identify talent. In ancient China, talented people were described as those who had ethics, magnanimity, abilities, aspirations, and accomplishments. Ethics generally refer to the ability to maintain personal integrity while engaged in political affairs. The current standard for ethics can be summarized with these words from Mao Zedong, "versed in Marxism-Leninism, politically far-sighted, competent in work, full of the spirit of self-sacrifice, capable of tackling problems on their own, steadfast in the midst of difficulties and loyal and devoted in serving the nation, the class and the Party."[27] Magnanimity refers to the ability to accept correct ideas and accommodate exceptional talent. Abilities refer to having creativity, knowing how to guide people and ideas, and being able to adapt to change. Aspirations refer to having lofty ideals, staunch determination, and tenacity. Accomplishments refer to achievements in one's official career. In other words, it describes people who dive into their work with enthusiasm and do their best to contribute to society. These leaders recognize that each person has their own role to play, and are committed to helping them live and work in peace.

Simply having a standard for identifying talent is not enough. We also need to have a method for recognizing talent. In "Assessing Others," a chapter from *The Annals of Lü Buwei*[28], people are evaluated based on "eight examinations and six tests."[29] The "eight examinations" include advice such as, "listen to their remarks and observe their conduct."[30] This is a very important point because some people like to exaggerate. Since their actions always fall short of their promises, they use phony gestures to try to handle other people. Leaders who choose to use "talent" like this will end up with a lot of headaches. One of the "six tests" suggests, "give them hard work in order to test their resolve." Such advice allows us to draw on a wealth of experience that we can then apply to our own work. Ningde is a poor place that needs dedicated people who are not afraid of really tough work. When we evaluate leaders, our emphasis is not on whether they can get amazing results right away, but on whether they have been dedicated to laying the groundwork for long-term projects. It is not realistic to think you can transform a poor place like Ningde overnight. However, if you give it your all and keep your nose to the grindstone, then you are the kind of talent we need.

Leaders need to be able to recommend talented people and use them wisely. The key is to recommend those who are virtuous and employ those who are capable. In other words, we should "recommend people on the basis of talent," and "appoint only those who are worthy." Some of the worst mistakes a leader can make are to "appoint people based on favoritism," assign rank according to seniority, and limit the talent pool to specific regions. In "Exalting Worthiness II," a volume from the *Mozi*[31], the author said that when wise rulers chose talented people, "...there were no factions with fathers and older brothers, no partiality towards the noble and rich, and no favouritism towards those of fine appearance."[32] In *Minglianglun*, Gong Zizhen[33] criticized government officials for giving out promotions based on seniority. In his *Memorial to the Throne Against the Expulsion of Guest Advisors*, Li Si[34] warned against the danger of only employing people from certain areas. His arguments were very insightful. I believe that the Chinese Communist Party has only one standard for choosing talent, the Four Criteria[35], which are applied to everyone based on merit. Regardless of where you call home, you will be promoted if you can satisfy the Four Criteria. Regardless of how much seniority you have, you will be promoted if you can get the job done right.

Leaders need to be able to judge a person's talents before awarding an appointment. Judging a person is similar to choosing a tool. We want to pick the one that is best suited to a project. Nevertheless, everyone has their strong and weak points[36], so we should not use rigid standards when judging talent. A steed that can run a thousand miles should not be made a poor plow horse, and a boat that can cross a river should not be stuck on land. Talent that is misplaced is apt to be wasted. When discussing the best way to make use of talent, Chen Yun[37] emphasized, "Try to make a perfect marriage between a person's talents and the work requirements. Employ talented people correctly and appoint them to suitable positions."

Leaders need to be able to respect a person's talents. This means respecting their individuality and creativity by not stifling or ignoring their abilities. It requires leaders to take an interest in talented people and value what they bring to the table. After all, we cannot expect a horse to run if we do not let it graze. Leaders must have confidence in their people. There is no point entrusting them with responsibilities only to mistreat them or express misgivings about them later. This will cause discord and dissension between leaders and the talented people who make up their teams. It is a recipe for disaster. The Tang Dynasty's Wei Zheng[38] said, "When a ruler wisely employs his subjects' talents, his subjects pledge complete loyalty to him.... A ruler who lacks confidence in his subjects cannot use them well. Subjects who lack confidence in their ruler cannot serve him well."[39] Although Wei

Zheng's remarks include some feudal ideas, we still can get valuable advice to apply to our own work.

Leaders need to be able to nurture talented people. In order to find worthy people, leaders must foster new talents. "A ruler who does not invest in educated men, yet seeks worthy subjects, is similar to an artisan who refuses to cut and polish a piece of jade, yet expects to find a beautifully decorated treasure."[40] I believe that mature leaders know how to cultivate talented people. They recognize that nurturing new talents is vital to ensuring that future generations have worthy leaders to advance our great cause. If leaders want to nurture talented people, they must take great pains to support them, enforce strict demands on them, and make bold use of them.

The self-cultivation of leaders

In ancient times, people described the standard for governing the country in a few short phrases, "One's character refined, the family in order, the nation governed, and the world at peace."[41] They believed that the ability of leaders to refine their character was so important they listed it first. Refining one's character is really just another way to say that leaders need to practice self-cultivation. In my opinion, this requires that leaders meet five conditions.

First, Party leaders must have the Party spirit. The spirit of the Communist Party of China is expressed when leaders serve the people with their whole heart. According to Karl Marx, the proletariat can only emancipate themselves when they have emancipated all humanity. The Communist Party of China is the political party of the proletariat. The nature of the Party determines that Party members must wholeheartedly serve the people. When leaders do this, they strengthen the Party spirit and meet the first condition for self-cultivation. If leaders do not have the Party spirit, then there is no point discussing anything else. The most effective way for leaders to strengthen the Party spirit is to go down to the grassroots and immerse themselves among the people. Lenin said, "And it is therefore our duty, if we wish to remain socialists to go down *lower and deeper*, to the real masses."[42] Going down to the grassroots and working shoulder-to-shoulder with the people are two of the most direct ways of serving them. Toward the end of 1988, I participated in a working conference of the Ningde prefectural Party committee, where we raised the idea of improving the leadership's way of work. Our ideas were later developed into the "four grassroots initiatives." The first initiative was to go down to the grassroots to publicize the Party's guideline, principles, and policies. The second initiative was to work with the grassroots to conduct investigations and research. The third initiative was to investigate complaints and listen to ideas at the grassroots level. The fourth initiative was to go down to the grassroots to handle official business on the spot. Many Party members are sent to extremely remote, impoverished areas, where they learn about the people's suffering firsthand. It has been a very moving experience. Upon their return, Party members always say that they have developed more empathy for the people, and they feel a stronger sense of responsibility to serve them. I believe that experiences like these strengthen the Party spirit and foster self-cultivation.

Second, Party leaders must be magnanimous. "A petty man is neither talented nor virtuous. A man of virtue is capable and brave."[43] To a certain extent, our successes in life are determined by our talents. Whether we make the most of our talents is determined by our magnanimity. Sima Guang said, "Efforts fail when authority is usurped. They succeed when there are joint efforts."[44] I believe these words offer much insight. When people usurp authority, they are being narrow-minded. When people are narrow-minded, they become separated from one another. And when people are separated from one another, they become destitute. However, when people make joint efforts, their world expands. When their world expands, obstacles are removed. And when obstacles are removed, people succeed. People who are narrow-minded stubbornly push their own agenda. They cannot accept reasonable ideas that are not their own, nor can they incorporate them to expand their own views. They act as though they have accomplished great deeds, but they are too afraid to employ the talented and virtuous to increase their own power. The fear that others will surpass them pushes narrow-minded people to attack and slander others in an attempt to raise themselves up. Communists, on the other hand, believe it is our responsibility to emancipate all humanity. Communists do not care about personal fame or fortune. We help others climb the ladder of success. We lay the groundwork for everyone else. The Party's mission and historical practice are a good starting point for anyone who would like to better understand this issue.

Third, Party leaders must have moral courage. A quick look at human history suggests that the people who accomplished great things were those who had great character. Karl Marx finished writing *Capital: A Critique of Political Economy* when he was at his most destitute. In February 1852, he wrote a letter to Engels saying, "A week ago I reached the pleasant point where I am unable to go out for want of the coats I have in pawn, and can no longer eat meat for want of credit."[45] Yet even then, Marx did not yield. He refused to stop working. Defying hardships while staying true to the doctrine shows the moral courage of a revolutionary proletariat. In ancient China, Confucius[46] praised the strong will of those people who refused to submit to brute force. He said, "The Three Armies may be stripped of their commander, but even a simple commoner cannot be deprived of his will."[47] Mencius[48] also offered guidance about the kind of integrity that is necessary to conduct oneself properly in the world. He suggested modeling ourselves on people who "cannot be led astray by riches and honor, moved by poverty and privation, or deflected by power or force."[49] I believe that moral courage is a quality every leader must have. Without it, leaders have no backbone. When talking about moral courage, we should be aware not to become dogmatic. A disciple of Confucius had the tassel on his helmet sliced off by his enemy while on the battlefield in the midst of a desperate fight. Believing this was an affront to his moral courage, the man lay down his arms to pick up the tassel. In that moment, he put more value on affixing the tassel, which symbolized his position as an official, than on fending off a fatal attack from the enemy. This is an example of dogmatism. Moral courage is called for when we talk about issues of principle. When we are faced with issues that do not involve principles, tactics should be the primary consideration.

Fourth, Party leaders must be honest. They need to speak honestly, work honestly, and act honestly. Do honest people usually get the short end of the stick? Some people think they do, but that is not how I see it. Seeking truth from facts lies at the very heart of Marxism. When we make a point of seeking truth from facts as we go about our lives, we speak honestly, work honestly, and act honestly. When we do not seek truth from facts, or we refuse to follow objective rules as we conduct our business, there may be times when we get the better of someone else, but ultimately we will run into problems and come out the loser. History has taught us that much. How do we speak honestly, work honestly, and act honestly? First, we always start with both feet firmly placed in reality. We respect the facts. We respect science. We stick out our necks to insist on the truth, and avoid being easily swayed when problems crop up. We refuse to offer blind obedience to our superiors or to believe only what we read in books. Instead, we start from the real situation on the ground. Second, we work more and talk less. Or perhaps we just work hard without boasting how dedicated we are. Our ancestors said that moral conduct is expressed through one's own actions; good reputation can only be confirmed when others recognize it. "One who is wise discriminates in his mind, but does not complicate his words. He exerts his strength, but does not brag about his achievement. In this way, his reputation and praise spread through the world."[50] People who exaggerate about their contributions and accomplishments will never develop a good reputation. Third, be honest in your dealings with people. If you can do that, leaders will want to employ you, colleagues will want to work with you, and subordinates will want to follow you.

Fifth, Party leaders must be bold. Their work is all-inclusive and ever changing. It demands that they are prepared to face an untold number of complicated situations. Leaders must be bold enough to cut to the heart of matters. If they hesitate all the time or fail to make decisions when they should, it will have a negative effect on their work. Nevertheless, leaders are not being bold when they make impulsive decisions divorcing them from objective laws. As Engels said, "Freedom of the will therefore means nothing but the capacity to make decisions with knowledge of the subject."[51] Leaders should cultivate boldness and exercise greater freedom of the will. The only way they can do this is by following Engels' advice – they need to go deep into the realities of life, and become knowledgeable about the outside world. This is the only way for leaders to properly handle complex issues in a bold and resolute manner.

For Communists, self-cultivation is not about sitting in meditation with our face toward the wall. Instead, it involves refining our actions and accumulating experience. As Communists, we don't view success as something handed down by immortal beings or gods. Instead, it is the inevitable result of practice. According to Marx, in remaking the world, the proletariat would remake themselves. As Communists, we strengthen self-cultivation and achieve success when we engage in the social practices of remaking the world. "The road to perfection requires constant practice. Constant practice yields sure success." Strengthening self-cultivation through practice and achieving success through practice are important principles. As Communists, we should abide by these principles so that we might make great contributions and accomplish great things.

Notes

[1] A native of Qiongshan, Guangdong Province (modern Haikou, Hainan Province), Hai Rui (1514-1587) served under four emperors in the Ming Dynasty (1368-1644). Known for his honesty, he is remembered as "Upright Official Hai."

[2] See "Eminence in Learning," in *Hanfeizi*. Born into the state of Han aristocracy, Han Fei (c. 280-233 BC) was a Legalist philosopher from the late Warring States Period whose life epitomized the Legalist school. His writings were collected into the book *Hanfeizi*. [Source of English translation: Han Fei Zi, "Eminence in Learning," in *Han Fei Tzu: Basic Writings*, trans. Burton Watson (New York: Columbia University Press, 1964), 108. – *Tr.*]

[3] This expression is from the "Biography of Gong Sui" in *History of the Han*. Compiled by the Eastern Han Dynasty's Ban Gu, *History of the Han* was the first Chinese work to record the history of a single dynasty through biographies. It is an important reference for studying the history of the Western Han Dynasty (1046-771 BC).

[4] This expression comes from "The 12 Hills," in *Weiliaozi*. Written by Wei Liao during the Warring States Period, *Weiliaozi* is an ancient military text that developed ideas from works such as Sun Tzu's *The Art of War* and the *Wuzi*. It has had a great influence on later generations.

[5] This is based on the following line from Qu Yuan's "The Fisherman," in *Verses of Chu*, "'Because all the world is muddy and I alone am clear,' said Qu Yuan, 'and because all men are drunk and I alone am sober, I have been sent into exile.'" [Source of English translation: Qu Yuan (340-278 BC), "Li Sao" ("On Encountering Trouble"), in *The Songs of the South*, trans. David Hawkes (Harmondsworth: Penguin Books Ltd., 2011), 70. – *Tr.*] Compiled by the Western Han Dynasty's Liu Xiang, *Verses of Chu* is a comprehensive anthology that focuses heavily on Qu Yuan's writings and includes similar works by other authors. Its distinctive literary style, use of dialects, and depiction of local customs imbues *Verses of Chu* with a strong sense of place.

[6] See Su Shi, "The Fourth Tactic."

[7] See Su Shi, "Edict Appointing Chen Tong the Minister of Shan Prefecture."

[8] Krikun was the name of a journalist in Alexander Korneychuk's play *Frontline* (1942). The character created news by reporting rumors and making up stories. Over the years, people have invoked his name to refer to this particular kind of journalism.

[9] A native of Xiangshan (modern Zhongshan), Guangdong Province, Sun Yat-sen (1866-1925) was the forerunner of democratic revolution in China. He proposed the Three Principles of the People, which can be summarized as national-

ism, democracy, and the livelihood of the people. He led the 1911 Revolution that overthrew the autocratic system that had ruled China for thousands of years. Later, he reorganized the Kuomintang, and implemented three major policies: unite with Russia, unite with the Communists, and support farmers and workers. He facilitated Kuomintang-Communist cooperation and advanced the democratic revolution against imperialism and feudalism.

[10] See chapter 63 of *Dao De Jing*. [Source of English translation: Lao Zi, *Tao Te Ching*, trans. D.C. Lau (Harmondsworth: Penguin Books Ltd, 1972), 124. –*Tr.*]

[11] A native of the state of Zhao, Xun Zi (c. 325-238 BC) was a philosopher, thinker, and educator of the late Warring States Period (475-221 BC). He believed that "the course of nature is constant," and proposed that people, who are born evil, controlled their own fate by "regulating what Heaven has mandated and using it." [Xun Zi, *Xunzi: A Translation and Study of the Complete Works,* trans. John Knoblock (Stanford: Stanford University Press, 1972), 7 & 21. – *Tr.*] His book *Xunzi,* was the first to summarize and develop the philosophical ideologies of Confucianism, Daoism, and Mohism in the pre-Qin (221-207 BC) period.

[12] Source of English translation: Xun Zi, "Book 11: Of Kings and Lords-Protector," in *Xunzi: A Translation and Study of the Complete Works*, vol. 2, trans. John Knoblock (Stanford: Stanford University Press, 1972), 149. –*Tr.*

[13] The Tang Dynasty's Li Bai (701-762), whose family was from Chengji, Longxi (southwest of modern Jingning, Gansu Province), was born in Suyab (now in northern Kyrgyzstan). He wrote with a unique style and romanticism that had not been seen since Qu Yuan. He was one of the greatest poets of his time in an era considered the golden age of China.

[14] Du Fu (712-770) was a Tang Dynasty poet. His ancestral home was Xiangyang, Hubei Province, and he is believed to have been born in Gong County (southwest of modern Gongyi, Henan Province). He made a point of reflecting social realities in his poems, further developing a literary tradition that had existed since *The Book of Songs*. His poetry stands out as one of the greatest artistic achievements in ancient China. After the Song Dynasty, he was honored with the title "Poet Sage," and has had a profound influence on the generations of poets who followed him.

[15] Li Bing was a water conservancy specialist who lived during the Warring States Period. He served as governor of Shu Prefecture from 256 to 251 BC, when he requisitioned laborers to work on irrigation projects that he initiated in the Min River basin. He is most famous for the Dujiangyan Irrigation System, which he built with his son. More than 2,200 years later, the benefits brought about by this feat of engineering are still evident on the western Sichuan plain. Later generations commemorated Li Bing and his son by building Two-King Temple at the Dujiang Dam, which is celebrated for its landscapes and historic sites.

[16] A craftsman from the Sui Dynasty, Li Chun built the Zhaozhou Bridge be-

tween 581-618. Structurally unique, this graceful bridge still stands as a marvel of architecture more than 1,500 years later.

[17] Lu Ban (507-444 BC) also known as Gongshu Ban, was a craftsman and builder in the Spring and Autumn Period. He took his surname from his home, the state of Lu. He invented the scaling ladder, which could be used to attack a city, developed a mill to grind powder, and is believed to have invented many tools used in carpentry. Later generations have held him up as the founder of carpentry and construction.

[18] Huang Daopo (1245-1330) also known as Huang Po, was from Wunijing, Songjiang (modern Dongwan, Xuhui, Shanghai). She is known for the technological innovations she made in the textile industry during the Yuan Dynasty (1206-1368).

[19] Source of English translation: Mao Zedong, "Speech at the Assembly of Representative of the Shaanxi-Kansu-Ningxia Border Region," in *Selected Works of Mao Tsetung*, vol. 3 (Beijing: Foreign Language Press, 1965), 33. – *Tr.*

[20] Chen Yi (1901-1972) was a Chinese proletarian revolutionary, military strategist, political leader and diplomat. He co-founded and commanded the Chinese People's Liberation Army and was the Marshal of the People's Republic of China.

[21] See Su Shi, "Two Prose Poems on the Red Cliff." [Source of English translation: Su Shi, "Two Prose Poems on the Red Cliff," in *Selected Poems of Su Tung-p'o*, trans. Burton Watson (Port Townsend: Copper Canyon Press, 1994), 96. – *Tr.*]

[22] Source of English translation: Friedrich Engels, *The Origin of the Family, Private Property and the State*, trans. Alec West (New York: International Publishers, 1975), 204. – *Tr.*

[23] *Ibid. – Tr.*

[24] Bao Zheng (999-1062) was from Hefei, Luzhou (now part of Anhui Province). An upright official with a quick mind for justice, he had a reputation for strictly enforcing the law and was the epitome of an honest official in ancient China. He lived in the Northern Song Dynasty, yet his deeds have been preserved for centuries in the form of popularly known stories and operas.

[25] See Bao Zheng, "Memorial to the Emperor."

[26] Source of English translation: Vladimir Lenin, "To A. D. Tsyurupa: A Programme for Work on New Lines," in *Collected Works*, vol. 35 (Moscow: Progress Publishers, 1973), 538-9. – *Tr.*

[27] Source of English translation: Mao Zedong, "Win the Masses in their Millions for the Anti-Japanese National United Front," in *Selected Works of Mao Tsetung*, vol. 1 (Beijing: Foreign Language Press, 1965), 291. – *Tr.*

[28] A native of Puyang in the state of Wei (modern Anyang, Henan Province), Lü Buwei (292-235 BC) was a well-known merchant and politician from the late Warring States Period (475-221BC). He summoned scholars to compile *The Annals of*

Lü Buwei, a comprehensive text that combined teachings from various schools of thought. The subject matter was drawn primarily from Confucian and Daoist philosophy, but also included ideas from Logicians, Legalists, Mohists, Agriculturists, and the School of Naturalists. *The Annals of Lü Buwei* became an ideological tool that the Qin state used to unify and govern the land.

[29] This is a method that rulers used to evaluate their subjects. It refers to eight types of conduct and six ways to observe behavior. [Source of English translation: Lü Buwei, "Book 3: 4 Lun Ren" in *The Annals of Lü Buwei,* trans. John Knoblock and Jeffrey Riegel (Stanford: Stanford University Press, 2000), 109. – *Tr.*]

[30] Source of English translation: Confucius, "Book Five," in *The Analects of Confucius,* trans. Burton Watson (New York: Columbia University Press, 2007), 37. – *Tr.*

[31] The *Mozi* is a compilation of writings from the Mohist school of thought. It is the primary reference for any study of Mo Zi and Mohism.

[32] Source of English translation: Mo Zi, "Exalting Worthiness II," in *The Mozi: A Complete Translation,* trans. Ian Johnston (New York: Columbia University Press, 2000), 63. – *Tr.*

[33] A native of Renhe (modern Hangzhou), Zhejiang Province, Gong Zizhen (1792-1841) was a thinker and writer from the Qing Dynasty (1644-1911).

[34] A native of Shangcai in the state of Chu (modern Henan Province), Li Si (?-208 BC) was a statesman of the Qin Dynasty (221-207 BC).

[35] In order to meet the "Four Criteria," officials should be revolutionary, young, knowledgeable, and professional.

[36] See Qu Yuan, "Bu Ju (Divination)," in *Verses of Chu.*

[37] A native of Qingpu (now part of Shanghai), Jiangsu Province, Chen Yun (1905-1995) was a Marxist, Chinese proletarian revolutionary, and statesman. He was one of the principal leaders of the Communist Party of China and the People's Republic of China. He was one of the architects who laid the foundation for socialist economic construction in China.

[38] A native of Julu Prefecture (modern Hebei Province), Wei Zheng (580-643) was a statesman of the early Tang Dynasty. His words are recorded in *Essentials of Government of the Zhenguan Reign.*

[39] See "Sincerity and Honesty," in *Essentials of Government of the Zhenguan Reign.* Compiled by the Tang Dynasty's Wu Jing, this text was published during the reign of Emperor Xuanzong.

[40] See Dong Zhongshu, "The Second Strategy," in *The Strategies to Elevate the Worthy.*

[41] See *The Great Learning* in *The Book of Rites.*

[42] Source of English translation: Vladimir Lenin, "Imperialism and the Split in Socialism," in *Collected Works,* vol. 23 (Moscow: Progress Publishers, 1974), 120. – *Tr.*

[43] See Anonymous (from the Song Dynasty), *Collection of Writings of Famous Worthies.*

[44] See Sima Guang (1019-1086), *Preface to The Argument for Great Achievements Through Joint Efforts.*

[45] Source of English translation: Karl Marx, "Letter from Marx to Engels, 27 February," in *Karl Marx, Fredrick Engels: Collected Works,* vol. 39 (New York: International Publishers, 1983), 50. – *Tr.*

[46] A native of Zou, in the state of Lu (modern Qufu, Shandong Province), Confucius (551-479 BC) was a thinker, educator, and statesman of the late Spring and Autumn Period (770-476 BC). The founder of Confucianism, he created a school of thought with benevolence at its core, and conceived of an ideology rich in philosophical wisdom. Dedicated to education, he compiled ancient texts, including *Classic of Poetry* and *Classic of Documents,* and revised the *Spring and Autumn Annals. The Analects of Confucius* is a collection of his theories and ideas. Known by emperors as the "Sage," his teachings have helped shape traditional Chinese culture for more than 2,000 years.

[47] This is a line from "Book Nine," in *The Analects of Confucius.* [Source of English translation: Confucius, "Book Nine," in *The Analects of Confucius,* trans. Burton Watson (New York: Columbia University Press, 2007), 63. – *Tr.*]

[48] A native of the state of Zou (modern Zou City, Shandong Province), Mencius (c. 372-289 BC) was a thinker, philosopher, and educator of the Warring States Period (475-221 BC). He maintained that man is an integral part of nature, proposed that human nature is good, and identified four cardinal virtues: benevolence, righteousness, propriety, and wisdom. He further developed the Confucian concepts of benevolence and "rule by virtue," and proposed that subjects were more important than their rulers. For defending Confucian principles and developing Confucian orthodoxy, he is called the "Second Sage" of Confucianism. The *Mencius* is a compilation of anecdotes and open discussions between Mencius and his disciples.

[49] This is a line from "Book 3B," in *Mencius.* [Source of English translation: Mencius, "Book 3B," in *Mencius,* trans. Irene Bloom (New York: Columbia University Press, 2009), 62. – *Tr.*]

[50] This is a line from "On Cultivating the Self," in the *Mozi.* The *Mozi* was written and compiled by followers of the Mohist school. [Source of English translation: Mo Zi, "On Cultivating the Self," in *The Mozi: A Complete Translation,* trans. Ian Johnston (New York: Columbia University Press, 2010), 13. – *Tr.*]

[51] Source of English translation: Friedrich Engels, *Herr Eugen Dühring's Revolution in Science,* trans. Emile Burns (New York: International Publishers, 1966), 125. – *Tr.*

The Nature of a Secretary's Work

– An Intimate Discussion with Officials in Prefecture and County General Offices

March 1990

The general office is a key department within a unit, system, and organ. How the work of general offices is conducted has a great impact on the work of the Party committees and even an entire region. Therefore, leaders in every location are concerned with and show great care for the work of their general office. "Planning takes place within the tents of command, victory is achieved thousands of miles away."[1] If the general office is well run, we can guarantee that all work will be smoothly carried out.

1. Four characteristics of office work

I previously worked as a secretary in the General Office of the Central Military Commission, so I am a colleague of you all. I later worked in county, city, and prefecture Party committees and governments, and I am intimately familiar with their relationships to their general offices. From my experiences, I have learned that there are four words that best describe the work of the general office:

First is "important" – the position is an important one. The work of the general office can be summed up in three parts: playing a policy advisory and brain trust role; serving those both above and below them; and secret and confidential work. All of these are important tasks. In 1975 Deng Xiaoping said while talking about rectification that these people are critical to the work in any given place: director of the general office, chief of the public security bureau, and head of the organization department. This shows the importance of the work of the general office. Since it advises decision-making, the general office always works closely with the leading authorities. When done well, advisory work can advance the smooth implementation of Party principles and policies. When not done well, it will impact the big picture and even lead to serious consequences. Within a work unit, the general office is the gatekeeper for the core secrets of leading authorities, and any leaks will harm the Party and the nation. Even something like a leak of confidential personnel information from our prefecture would impact the unity of the leadership and stir up emotions. The general office also serves as "a window" to the outside. The impressions grassroots officials and visiting officials make of our prefecture and leaders are related, to a great extent, to the work of the general office. When the quality of work is outstanding, people will say that this place does good work. If office personnel do sloppy work or take on brash attitudes, people will think that the work done in this place must be a mess. Therefore, the work of the general office is closely related to the overall work.

Second is "hard" – office work is not a walk in the park. Everyone working in the general office experiences hardships, with in-trays that are never empty, frequent calls to work overtime, and even working through the night. Even the arrival of Saturday does not guarantee free time. Secretaries rushing to meet deadlines have it even harder, as their work is extremely intense and the workload is particularly burdensome. Liu Zhen[2] of the Eastern Han Dynasty described such work vividly in a poem, "Writing all day without stopping to eat, skipping dinner when the sun goes down; after burying my head in books all day, I return home with eyes in a daze." Such is a secretary's life.

Third is "complex" – the job is quite complicated. Work in the general office ranges all the way from top-level affairs of state and important decisions to indoor sanitation and officials' welfare, from receiving top leaders to contacting ordinary citizens, and from the innermost secrets to public sentiments – everything is fair game. Internal work may cover things such as research, information, investigations, petitions, reception, classified information, archiving, printing, and dispatching. Office officials have to deal with several, dozens, and even hundreds of matters each day. We are constantly being pulled in every direction, and feel like what the poet said that "it is so beautiful on the Shanyin road that one can hardly catch all the scenes along the way."[3]

Fourth is "difficult" – the level of difficulty is quite high. The work of the general office is all-encompassing and open in every direction. We both have to manage relationships all around us, and also adapt to the leaders' work styles and methods and serve them well. There are a million things to take care of when it comes to implementing tasks assigned by leaders. Some of these things must be done immediately without delay, and some are continual, ongoing tasks that must be attended to at all times. It takes incredible concentration and a continual state of heightened awareness to determine what is most urgent and what can wait, and not overlook things or make mistakes. At the same time, the general office deals with many everyday affairs. When achievements are made, those of us who work in general offices do not receive credit and remain unsung heroes behind the scenes. When there are problems, we may become the focus of everyone's attention, which can make us run the gamut of emotions until the situation is resolved. Sometimes we will be blamed for others' mistakes and make accommodations for the sake of overall interests. This type of situation is truly difficult to deal with. In a sense, each task is a result of the hard work and dedication of our general office colleagues.

2. Three wishes for the work of general offices

How should we perform the work of general offices? All of you are the most qualified to speak on this subject. I can only express three wishes based on my own experiences and work.

My first wish: have a strong sense of responsibility. The work of the general office affects all work. This requires that all of our office colleagues have a strong initiative, earnest work attitude, and scrupulous work style. The work of the general office involves many secrets, and there are specific rules on where each document can and cannot go, which we must carefully follow. In particular, some matters involve political and economic intelligence, requiring from us an even greater sense of responsibility, habit of maintaining silence, and restraint from opening one's mouth where one shouldn't. The work must be done meticulously. As the old saying goes, "One word out of place can wreck the entire sentence; one mistaken sentence can throw off the entire passage."[4] Documents drafted in the general office don't need to be written in flowery language, but they must be carefully completed. This is not an over-the-top requirement, as it is directly related to decision-making. Therefore, we must train and employ workers who can deftly wield the pen, so the leaders don't have to wrack their brains for the right choice of words. This is a minimum requirement. Except when we are working under tight deadlines, all written materials we send to our leaders to look over must be a clean copy. We cannot look on this as being additional work. If all sorts of revisions are made on a messy draft for which we cannot tell who made the final revision, no one can be held responsible for the final document. Therefore, we must have a strict manner of work that has a high degree of responsibility and strong sense of initiative.

The general office is the main organ of a work unit, and it must always be acting as a model for the entire unit. It must pay attention to all aspects of work, including reception, sanitation, and impressions it makes on people. As part of the office, secretaries of leading officials often relay the leaders' intentions and handle matters on their behalf. Their quality and manner of work directly reflects the spirit and appearance of the leading organ. Therefore, the general office must care about the political and work performance of these secretaries. The general office should make sure that they receive criticism for poor performance, and that they frequently report on their thoughts and work. Secretaries serve the leaders out of a need for their work and do not have any political privileges. On the whole, the general office is a complete machine. This machine requires a clear responsibility system, strict management, and sensible measures, so those of us working in it will know our position, act within the rules, perform our given duties, and take up our responsibilities. We must react nimbly, operate quickly, and adapt to the needs of all sides.

My second wish: work with high efficiency. The general office has to handle many, many tasks each day and resolve conflicts and problems in all sorts of places. This means that we must always be improving our work efficiency. Otherwise we will not be able to properly provide the "three services,"[5] and this will impact the work in general of the entire prefecture. To improve our work efficiency, I believe that we must learn to apply dialectics, be clear about priorities, and earnestly reflect. We must "plan based on importance, arrange based on urgency, connect with above and below, and balance between internal and external."[6] That is, we must make use of the office as a whole, consider what affairs are major and urgent, always keep our eye on matters of great importance, and get a handle on urgent tasks first. We must communicate with those all around us, let those below us know what is happening above, and remember the difference between the internal and external. All tasks must be properly assessed and methodically completed.

Another important job that the general office performs is in its advisory role. The office is expected to promptly provide policy recommendations and solidify leaders' decisions into concrete opinions. If our office can analyze situations from every angle just like foreign "thinktanks" do, and frequently offer suggestions for major policy decisions, it can greatly help the leaders to make decisions and choices. Currently, there are many tough problems and hot-button issues in our economic development and social work. They require us to conduct thorough investigation and research, provide targeted measures for analyzing and resolving problems, and offer leaders at all levels valuable policy references.

My third wish: provide high-level service. Providing service is an important job of the general office. First, I want to emphasize the notion of providing service both before and after events occur. For example, when an important prefecture and county meeting is held, staff in the general office must get in place beforehand. In particular, the office director, meeting secretary, and extra office hands must arrive early to prepare for the meeting. After the meeting, they must write up minutes and documents, and check up on implementation and feedback. Next, the service must be prompt and thorough. The general office must help share the burden of our leaders. Third, our service must take full responsibility and leave nothing overlooked. For example, when our office runs on a strict 24-hour schedule, those on duty cannot leave even for a minute. If an emergency or major incident suddenly occurs while the office is empty, lack of timely response will not only be considered negligence, but also have consequences. Fourth, our service not only must be diligent and earnest, but also agile. For example, we must put forth our best effort when receiving guests. We should establish a set of guidelines for reception, organize a hospitality team, and prepare consistent promotional materials and reports. Going forward, we can have designated officials responsible for reporting and accompanying visits. Meals can feature local products and traditions as long as they comply with applicable standards. Each county can prepare its own local menu that is both unique and economical. In this way, everyone can enjoy a good meal and learn about the local food culture within the limits set by the standards. Why not show our hospitality with such a simple gesture? Prefecture and county leaders should attend events in accordance with the rules and reduce participation in mere courtesy events to the extent possible. Those involved in reception work should serve the guests with warmth and consideration: put yourself in their shoes, think about what they will need, and help resolve their problems.

3. Office secretaries should strengthen self-cultivation

Secretary is a special profession. Many people believe that the most prominent feature of a secretary's work is serving in a support-ive role like a supporting actor. I think this is both right and wrong. It is right in that a secretary truly does supportive and foundational work as the leader's assistant. It is wrong in that a secretary has even less space than a supporting actor on the stage, as the secretary has no spoken lines or opportunities to share the spotlight. The nature of the secretary's work means that he/she must have the proper attitude toward fame, fortune, and honor, with a selfless spirit, and continually strengthen self-cultivation.

How can secretaries strengthen their self-cultivation? During the Song Dynasty, Lü Benzhong[7], in his famous *Admonishments to Offi-cials*, argued that all officials must be clean, prudent, and diligent. I think that if we update his ideas for today's age, they can serve as the minimum requirements for staff in the general office, in particu-lar secretaries to leading officials. To be "clean" means to act with integrity and have nothing to hide. To be "prudent" means to give careful consideration and be cautious in words and deeds. To be "dili-gent" means to study hard and do our best to advance. Of course, these three requirements must be met while remaining politically and ideologically faithful to the Party Central Committee. Secretaries must always be studying – studying Marxism-Leninism, Mao Zedong Thought, Party guideline, principles, and policies, and the issues of our times. In this way, we can continually deepen our understanding of theories and improve our political qualities.

Given the special nature of the work of a secretary, it is not enough just to work hard. I personally have experienced that secretar-ies must not only strengthen self-cultivation, but also focus on devel-oping good manner of work, take note of the little details in personal life, and strive to stay away from five things:

First, don't be self-conceited. We cannot mistakenly believe that we have nothing to fear just because "our organization has a big name and our leaders will back us up," nor can we allow the misuse of the names of our leaders and of the office to seek out personal profit.

Second, don't be arrogant. We must check our sense of superiority, and never be domineering, arrogant, bossy, or commanding with grassroots officials and people.

Third, don't be boastful. We must not show off or brag. When it comes to the work and personal life of a leader, we cannot discuss it publicly or make presumptuous comments. And a tight lid must be kept on internal Party secrets.

Fourth, don't be ashamed of yourself. We must overcome the urge to underestimate ourselves or feel like we are not up to the task. We cannot "open our mouths only to stutter, and take a step only to stumble." We cannot be mindless yes-men with no views of our own.

Fifth, don't get a big head. We must not think we have all the answers and change or add our own views to our leaders' instructions. We cannot be careless, do the bare minimum to get by, or not take our duties seriously.

In general, secretaries must frequently check whether our own thinking and work are "in position"–it cannot "be misplaced" or "overreach." In our relationships with our leaders, we must strive to "participate and not interfere, assist and not exceed our authority, and comply but not follow blindly." I believe that as long as we are always clear about our own position, we can become secretaries fully qualified for the job.

4. Prefecture and county Party committees must support general offices

Local Party committee leaders must understand, trust, and respect the work of the general office in order to truly support and make full use of it.

First, due attention must be given to the Party committee's work on the general office. Prefecture and county Party committees must hold special meetings each year to discuss the work of their general offices and help them resolve actual problems. Leading officials of prefecture and county Party committees should frequently communicate with the staff of the general office to share thoughts, discuss work, and listen to everyone's opinions and suggestions.

Second, leaders must involve themselves with office team building. Now we are facing the difficulties of selecting, transferring, and promoting officials in relation to the general office. By "difficulty of selecting," I mean it is hard to find candidates with superior political qualities and writing skills. Even when we do find good candidates, it is still difficult to get them to work in our general offices for various reasons – this is the "difficulty of transferring." Due to the limited number of job openings, it is also difficult to promote officials who have worked hard in the general office for a long time, who diligently do their jobs without complaint, and who perform exceptionally well. Our leaders must be determined to resolve these problems. One measure to take is to set strict entrance and exit criteria. We cannot compromise on the criteria for new hires. Incoming colleagues must be politically reliable and of excellent character. I want to stress that we must be able to transfer suitable people within our prefecture as we deem fit. To truly resolve the problem of difficulties in selection and transfers, there should be no bargaining or restrictions by department or locality. Personnel departments must also boldly promote and employ qualified office officials and resolve the issue of office personnel hanging around in the same positions for too long. We cannot afford to play favorites in general offices; those who are not suited to such work should immediately be transferred out. If office personnel have lax work attitudes, take too many liberties, and have poor political and professional qualities, the image of Party committees will suffer. Leading officials of prefecture and county Party committees should be informed about key personnel changes in general offices. On the whole, we must step up office team building and ensure that staff bring vigor to their office work so that general offices continue to run effectively.

Third, leaders must show concern for the learning, life, and political progress of our office colleagues. On the one hand, we must create favorable conditions for all who work in general offices, including organizing study sessions and tours out of the office, as we can only improve the level of our policies by gaining a better understanding of the situation outside the office. Office work is fast-paced, but we still must schedule study sessions and let our colleagues in general offices step away from their desks for new learning. On the other hand, we must also acknowledge the hardships office staff encounter in their lives. On top of performing hard work on the job, our colleagues in general offices lead very plain lives and their families often have unmet needs. However, these colleagues have made the conscious choice of dedicating themselves to the Party, taking on responsibility for their work and making contributions behind the scene. Such a choice of theirs is all the more reason for our leaders to recognize the sacrifices of our colleagues working in general offices. In particular, leaders should do their best to help address concerns that our office colleagues have about schooling for their children, housing, and other difficulties in their lives, so such problems will not come back to bite us in the end.

Notes

[1] See Sima Qian (145-90 BC), "The Basic Annals of Emperor Gaozu," in *Records of the Grand Historian*.

[2] A native of Ningyang, Dongping (modern Shandong Province), Liu Zhen (186-217) was a scholar of the Eastern Han Dynasty (25-220). He was one of the seven leading writers from the Jian'an Period.

[3] This is based on the following line from "Speech and Conversation," in *A New Account of Tales of the World* by the Song Dynasty's Liu Yiqing, "Whenever I travel by the Shanyin road, the hills and streams naturally complement each other in such a way that I can't begin to describe them. And especially if it's at the turning point between autumn and winter, I find it all the harder to express what's in my heart." [Source of English translation: Liu Yiqing, *A New Account of Tales of the World*, trans. Richard B. Mather (Minneapolis: University of Minnesota Press, 1976), 71. Mather's English translation was revised to be consistent with the rest of the text. – Tr.]

[4] This is a line from Liu Qi's preface to *Compendium of Auxiliary Characters*, a highly technical reference for the study of grammatical function words in ancient Chinese texts. It was first printed in 1711, during the reign of Emperor Kangxi.

[5] At a national symposium for senior Party secretaries from general offices held in 1985, the director of the General Office of the CPC Central Committee, Wang

Zhaoguo, put forward the concept of the "three services," which are serving the leadership, serving government offices at all levels, and serving the people.

[6] See Feng Menglong, "Chapter 26," *Chronicles of the Eastern Zhou Kingdoms*. A native of Changzhou (modern Suzhou, Jiangsu Province), Feng Menglong (1574-1646) was a writer and dramatist of the Ming Dynasty (1368-1644). He was dedicated to studying, organizing, and writing popular literature such as novels and operas.

[7] A native of Shou Prefecture (modern Fengtai, Anhui Province), Lü Benzhong (1084-1145) was a poet of the Southern Song Dynasty (1127-1279).

Water Droplets Drilling Through Rock

March 1990

Upon settling in the countryside, I saw firsthand the power of dripping water drilling through rock. That image, which captured the spirit of persistence, has stayed with me all these years. It has become a well-worn source for contemplating life and movement.

Rock and water are two opposing elements that are used to symbolize dogged stubbornness and gentle fluidity. Yet despite being "gentle," water will drill through "solid" rock over time.

As a metaphor for people, this is the embodiment of a certain moral character: it is the willingness to rise to fight each time one falls and the courage to sacrifice oneself. A single drop of water is small and insubstantial. It will die a cruel "death" in any battle with a rock. Yet in that brief moment of "sacrifice," even though it cannot see its own value and achievement, it is embodied within the countless drops of water that have already fallen, and the triumph of finally drilling through the rock. From the perspective of history or development of an economically disadvantaged area, we should not seek personal success and fame. Instead, we should strive to make steady progress one small step at a time and be willing to lay the groundwork for overall success. When everyone doing our work models themselves on a droplet that is ready to sacrifice for the greater good, we need not worry that our work is not important enough to make lasting change!

As a metaphor for things, dripping water is a demonstration of dialectical principles that use softness to overcome hardness, and the weak to control the strong. I believe in the invaluable spirit of that drop of water, which bravely goes into the breach with no thought of retreat. Those of us who are involved in economic development will inevitably encounter complications in our work. We can either rise to the challenge or flinch and run away. It all depends on whether we have the courage to adhere to philosophical materialism. If we allow ourselves to be filled with trepidation, the kind of fear that comes from standing at the edge of an abyss or treading on thin ice, we will lack the courage to do anything. We will accomplish nothing. Nevertheless, courage alone is not enough.

When dripping water takes aim at a rock, each droplet zeroes in on the same target and stays the course until its mission is complete. The drops of water fall day after day, year after year. This is the magic that enables dripping water to drill through rock! How can it be that our economic development work is any different? Just look at areas where the economy is lagging. Historical, environmental, and geographical factors have all played a part in holding back development. There are no shortcuts. Nothing can change overnight. Instead, we need to focus on the long haul by turning quantitative changes into qualitative changes. We need to be the dripping water that drills through rock. When talking about reform and opening up, we cannot assume that help will be coming from left and right, nor can we afford to wait until conditions are perfect enough to ensure success. Instead of building palaces in the air, we need to square our shoulders and get down to work. When talking about economic development, we cannot simply race to build high-rises and open up big factories, nor can we focus on dramatic results at the expense of necessary infrastructure. Otherwise, success will be elusive, and opportunities will be easily missed.

Instead of daydreaming about overly ambitious or flashy projects, we need to have a firm footing in reality as we take concrete steps to reach long-term goals. Instead of "setting three fires" in the hope they will succeed, we need to work steadily and make solid progress. Our work calls for the tenacity to keep chipping away. Working by fits and starts will not get us anywhere.

When I describe my awe upon seeing the power of droplets drilling through rock, I am praising those who have the willingness to rise each time one falls, and the moral character to sacrifice for overall success. I am expressing my admiration for those who develop a solid plan and then have the tenacity to see it through to the end.

Always Keeping the People in Mind
– On Handling Petition Work in the New Situation

April 1990

Petition departments are the bridges linking the Party and government with the people, as well as the windows opening to the sentiments of the people. Chen Zi'ang of the Tang Dynasty wrote in a poem: "The sage does not look to benefit himself, he worries for and aids the common folk."[1] That is, virtuous people do not pursue advantage for themselves, and instead they care about and help the ordinary people. It would have been quite an achievement for the grand ministers of China's dynastic ages to have such a view, but they still saw themselves as "sages" and saviors and still had the attitude of looking down upon the people from on high. In contrast, we Communist Party officials come from the people and are here for the people. In petition work it is both our responsibility and obligation to listen to the voices of the people, understand their wishes, improve our work and work manner constantly, and care for and aid every person who needs it. The principal aim of petition work is always seeing ourselves as one of the people and always keeping the people in mind.

In essence, petition work refers to handling letters sent from the people and receiving people who have come to visit. Governments at all levels within the prefecture and counties of Ningde have established a visit appointment system and set dates for leaders to receive visitors. Is it enough then if we simply reply to all letters and receive all visitors? I think not, because this is simply a passive attitude toward petition work, and there is still a gap between the requirements for the work in the new era and the people's hopes for all levels of leadership. In the new situation leaders at all levels need to stop putting on airs, get rid of bureaucratism, and find time to visit people. Thus they may carry out the petition work at the grassroots level and bring the care of the Party and aid of the government into the homes of ordinary people.

Leaders can improve their work manner and overcome bureaucratism by leaving office and making visits to people. As Lenin incisively pointed out, "In the sea of people we are after all but a drop in the ocean, and we can administer only when we express correctly what the people are conscious of."[2] However, some of our leading officials have truly forgotten our fine tradition of linking with the people, misunderstood the very meaning of Party leadership, and gotten used to issuing orders from above. Some of our other colleagues cannot extricate themselves from the "mountains of papers and seas of meetings." They seldom make it to the grassroots level, and this forms a barrier that keeps the people away. When this is the case, the opinions and needs of the people do not reach the leaders in time, and Party and government policies and decisions also cannot be effectively implemented.

While visiting the people, leaders at all levels should "watch what they do, find out how much they make, and examine where they live"[3] to learn about their work and life conditions. This can fundamentally prevent the bad habits of authoritarianism and bureaucratism. We believe that leaders at all levels should go to the grassroots with their tasks and problems and closely examine practical cases. Delving deep into the grassroots and improving the work efficiency of leading authorities help with resolving problems at the source and defusing conflicts in their budding stages. At the same time, we must actively educate the people, promote our policies among them, and improve the work manner at all levels of leadership. In this way, Party principles and policies will be fully implemented.

By visiting the people, leaders can have a better relationship with the people and build up a strong notion of serving the people with

heart and soul. No matter how senior they are, leaders at prefecture and county levels are the servants of the people and must have
the comfort and safety of the people in mind. "Governance lies in
reassuring the people; reassuring the people lies in observing their
suffering."[4] The exemplary Party official Jiao Yulu[5] often went to the
villages and into households where the poorest and most hard-off
people lived. He took the county Party committee members to the
train station where people were fleeing from famine. And when there
was a huge snowfall, he had the county officials visit homes of farmers to help them solve problems. He stooped into low thatched huts,
sat with farmers at their bedsides, and told them he was the son of a
farmer himself. Like the county where Jiao Yulu worked, Ningde is
also an impoverished region, and all Party members and officials, in
particular those with leadership responsibilities, should think carefully
about how they measure up to Jiao Yulu. We should often consider
whether we are "completely" and "thoroughly" serving the people,
and what we have done for the people and what problems we have
resolved within the scope of our own duties. We should consider
whether we are trying to outdo our neighbors in terms of "position,
wealth, house, wife, and children," or whether we are willing to roll
up our sleeves and toil alongside the people. We can only gain their
sincere support by keeping them in our minds and working to advance
their interest.

Leaders can hear the voices of the people and submit to their
supervision when visiting them in their homes. Since the reform and
opening up, the prefectures and counties have realized great achievements in all levels of work, but certain problems still exist. This
requires us to pay attention to the voices of the people and consciously submit to their criticism and supervision. We must promptly accept
the correct opinions of the people to drive our current work. When
given incorrect opinions, we must patiently and carefully explain
our thinking based on the situation. Some of our colleagues cannot
stand to hear the slightest criticism and aren't willing to perform self-
criticisms. Some engage in flattery, give people a hard time, seize upon

faults, or wield a big "stick" when people offer their opinions, and this is strictly forbidden under Party discipline. "What is the key to rapid success in establishing order? It is in treating people with the utmost sincerity." As long as leaders at all levels form true connections with the people, genuinely share their views, and persist in coming from the people and going to the people, our work will continue to improve, and our causes will thrive and grow.

Leaders also need to visit the people to unite them and stabilize the overall situation. As Deng Xiaoping[6] once said, why do the people follow the Communist Party? First is to rise up and be liberated, and second is to prosper and find happiness. After 40 years of construction, Ningde, like the rest of the country, has made huge achievements in economic and social development. But due to various reasons, the life of farmers in some mountainous counties and townships is still a far cry from "prosperity and happiness." When faced with the current fiscal difficulties in certain impoverished counties and townships, our colleagues cannot be like the poet who "heaves a long sigh and brushes away his tears, sad that man's life should be so beset with hardship."[7] Instead, they must actively work out plans, follow the feedback and needs of the people, work hard to get more done for them, and achieve solid, beneficial results. They must lay out the concept of beneficial, solid results: this includes supporting economic development and helping the people prosper; it also includes upholding social integrity, fighting those who would spoil our achievements, enriching the cultural life of the people, and creating a good social environment that is culturally advanced, friendly, harmonious, and stable. Furthermore, it includes resolving the people's difficulties in terms of clothing, food, housing, and transportation, and the people's needs during birth, old age, illness, and death. It even extends to us being able to care about and help with the small matters like people in remote mountainous areas not being able to buy everyday items such as light bulbs and soap. It is easy to say we will achieve solid results for the people, but it is difficult to actually pull it off. It is easy to achieve one result for one day, but it is hard to keep at it until the end. We must be clear about what is truly important and what is truly urgent. We must have the spirit of "water droplets drilling through rock" and keep plugging away without letting up in our efforts to make the people understand, come around to our side, be happy, and be satisfied.

Notes

[1] See Chen Zi'ang, "Poem 19," in *Stirred by My Experiences: A Series of 38 Poems.* A native of Shehong, Zi Prefecture (now part of Sichuan Province), Chen Zi'ang (659-700) was a writer of the Tang Dynasty (618-907). An early innovator of Tang Dynasty poetry, he had a significant influence on its development.

[2] Source of English translation: Vladimir Lenin, "Eleventh Congress of the R.C.P.(B.): Political Report of the C.C., R.C.P.(B.). in *Collected Works*, vol. 33 (Moscow: Progress Publishers, 1973), 304. – *Tr.*

[3] See "Book 2," in *The Analects of Confucius.*

[4] See Zhang Juzheng, "Memorial to the Emperor Proposing Taxes Be Waived to Reassure the People."

[5] A native of Zibo, Shandong Province, Jiao Yulu (1922-1964) was a model official of the Communist Party of China. He joined the Party in 1946, and was appointed county Party secretary of Lankao, Henan Province, in 1962.

[6] A native of Guang'an, Sichuan Province, Deng Xiaoping (1904-1997) was a Marxist, Chinese proletarian revolutionary, statesman, military strategist, and diplomat. He was one of the leaders of the Communist Party of China, the Chinese People's Liberation Army, and the People's Republic of China. The principal founder of Deng Xiaoping Theory, he was the chief architect of China's socialist reform and opening up and modernization drive.

[7] See Qu Yuan, "On Encountering Trouble." [Source of English translation (slightly revised here): Qu Yuan, "Li Sao (On Encountering Trouble)," in *The Songs of the South,* trans. David Hawkes (Harmondsworth: Penguin Books Ltd., 1985), 70. – *Tr.*]

Seize New Opportunities

October 1988

Rectification provides us with new opportunities

Reporter: In interviews, I heard some local officials and people talking about that the "yellow earth" coastal area of Ningde Prefecture had failed to catch up with the "last train" of great economic development for various reasons, and now when they are ready to join in the development but it is already too late. Some people therefore say with regret that time is not working in their favor. What do the prefecture's leaders think about this?

Xi Jinping: Now the country is focusing on rectification, and this truly does have an impact on the economic development of the Ningde Prefecture. But we also saw that rectification and improvement are similarly indispensable for economically underdeveloped regions. We used to regard Ningde Prefecture as a region at the front line. For nearly 40 years since the People's Republic was founded, state investment in this region only accounted for 4% of the amount invested in the province, and the prefectural economic foundations were quite weak. Despite the small scale of capital construction, there was overheating and disorder. There are still varying degrees of nonconformity to economic law such as blind investment, unclear thinking, and a rush to completion, and this is an impediment to developing the economy. Therefore, we must start rectification.

This is an interview with a reporter from *Economic Daily*, first published in *Economic Daily* on October 21, 1988.

However, I want to stress that rectification does not mean recalling or putting an end to reform. Instead, it creates good conditions for further reform and helps the economy develop smoothly and healthily. Therefore, rectification will not have a negative impact on the economy of our prefecture, but it will provide our economically underdeveloped region with new opportunities for development. Ningde Prefecture is mainly mountainous, and has poor industrial foundations. But it has fairly good agriculture, and we can say that we are in a good position to take advantage of the mountains and seas and to develop "big agriculture." Now the central authorities are trying to reduce overheating and overexpansion, and are driving the point home that the entire Party and country must give due attention to agriculture. These policies will favor our agricultural development. Therefore, this is a new opportunity for our prefectural development. Based on this awareness, in our overall prefectural development strategy, we are mainly focusing on developing agriculture and fully tapping mountain- and sea-based resources. We want to first develop the foundation of agriculture and make good use of our advantages in three areas: township enterprises; forests, tea, and fruits; and aquatic product production. Through the development of modern "big agriculture," farmers will come out of poverty to prosperity, our foundations will grow, and a production system suited to local conditions will be steadily established.

There's another point I want to mention: the main reason that Ningde Prefecture is economically underdeveloped is because it lacks electric power and has poor transportation. Without ample electric power there is no way we can develop industry and agriculture and open up to the outside world. We have rich hydroelectric resources here, and some small hydroelectric stations have been built, but run-of-the-river power generation is limited during the dry season. The country is currently adjusting its industrial structure and strengthening its energy, transportation, and raw material industries, so it is a good time for us to develop our power generation and transportation infrastructure. We are currently preparing to link up with the provincial grid and develop two medium-large hydroelectric plants to get our power issues resolved. Transportation is another issue, as we do not have railways through the region, and our roads don't meet high standards. The people complain of the shoddy quality of the roads[1]. We plan on improving the current standards of our roads through private initiatives with public assistance. The coastal Highway 104 will be upgraded section by section, and with key state support we aim to complete it in seven to eight years. We will also focus on wharf construction and program-control telephone systems with 10,000-line capacity. Building such infrastructure both conforms to the current requirement of rectification and lays the necessary foundation for the prefecture's economic development to take off in the future.

We must dilute the "poor-county mentality"

Reporter: There is truly much promise in this work you talk about, but some of our colleagues feel like they will always be one step behind Fuzhou and Xiamen and can't get excited about their work.

Xi Jinping: Fuzhou and Xiamen are both in plain regions. They are also centuries-old trading cities with good urban foundations and transportation conditions. We are in a mountainous region with starkly contrasting natural features, so we cannot blindly make unrealistic comparisons with other places. I was transferred here from Xiamen in June of this year, so I have experienced this myself. What is Xiamen all about? A development zone has been set up there, and the state has made a large investment of RMB3 billion. You are in for nothing but disappointment if you try to compare yourself with Xiamen.

Ningde Prefecture, on the other hand, has been named one of China's 18 impoverished regions; of its nine counties, six are impoverished. To be fair, life is pretty hard in some impoverished counties like Shouning and Pingnan. In other counties, they don't have it as rough as people joke about them being "impoverished counties where everyone wears a suit." I've had discussions with other leaders in the prefecture, and we have learned that "there are times… when a foot is too short, and there are times when an inch is too long" and "the pines and cypresses need not be envious of the peach and plum trees" – we are not inferior to others in every way. This is an old revolutionary soviet area with large minority populations. We are recognized as having impoverished counties and receive preferential policy treatment. On the one hand, our economy is underdeveloped. On the other hand, the state also shows its concern for the region. We must face up to this problem and not let poverty bring our spirits down.

Poor as we are, we shouldn't lose our lofty ideals. We mustn't get used to talking about how poor our county or prefecture is because our county is designated as an impoverished one. Over time we will see ourselves as inferior to others and lose spirit, and this sense of inferiority will lead to a "poor-county mentality." For example, people would not want to sit in the front row during provincial meetings, would wait until last to speak, and would not dare speak in a loud voice. I worry that the badge of being an "impoverished county" may give some people an undeserved "poor-county mentality," and this will affect our poverty alleviation work. Therefore, I want to rouse our spirits and pour cold water on such ways of thinking. On the one hand we must admit that conditions here are poor and the economy is backward. We cannot unrealistically compare ourselves with developed regions and compete with them in the number of mega projects and in the rate of development. On the other hand, we must see that this place is like every other place in China in that over the past 40 years it has truly made great strides and seen huge changes. For example, there is industry where there was none before, and we have formed a diversified industrial base with RMB1 billion of output that mainly produces light textiles while also featuring high-end, new, niche, and rare products. Our agriculture can hold its own against any other region in the province, and our culture, education, and public health have developed greatly. Such huge changes did not come overnight, and instead were like water droplets drilling through rock. They were achieved under poor conditions with little investment from the state – quite an accomplishment in itself. Recognizing our own achievements and strengths can bolster our confidence and self-respect, which will go a long way in helping us steadily march down the path of development.

We cannot wish for a sudden "gold mine"

Reporter: During our interviews we learned that officials and the people have a strong desire to move quickly out of poverty to prosperity, and they hope that some large projects such as railways, large ports, or development zones will fundamentally change the backwardness of this area overnight.

Xi Jinping: The three main economic topics of our prefecture are building a coastal railway from Fuzhou to Wenzhou, developing a 500,000-ton port at Sandu'ao, and creating the Saiqi Development Zone, which will eventually become a central city. Officials and the people urgently want to move out of poverty toward prosperity as soon as possible. This kind of desire is good, and such enthusiasm is valuable. But it is simply not realistic to place our hopes in huge projects and hope to suddenly be given a "gold mine."

Railways need huge funds to build, and it is up to the state planners to decide where and when to build them. That is not something we can just go and do ourselves. Of course, we can provide reasonable recommendations and work hard to promote the idea, but such a project will not be realized in the coming period. Development of the Sandu'ao port involves the issues of some old ports in Fujian still not running at full capacity and where limited state funds should be channeled. Ningde Prefecture is neither a central region nor a producer of raw materials or logistics center. These factors all restrict the building of railways and ports. As for turning the Saiqi Development Zone into a central city, this is no simple task. Central cities cannot be thrown up just anywhere, and instead must naturally be formed gradually through economic development. I threw some cold water on these three hot topics of conversation. That is, we cannot be impetuous, and we cannot hope for sudden miracles. Instead, I believe the correct path is to start from the actual local situation, make full use of current conditions, solidly build agriculture and other infrastructure, and gradually realize development. Of course, we must actively prepare for the big projects we just mentioned so we can do a proper job when the time is ripe. However, we cannot place our focus on things that we cannot accomplish right now. The same goes for opening up to the outside world. Even though this is located at the opening-up coastal belt, its foundations are the weakest, and it has many disadvantageous conditions for attracting foreign capital, so we cannot compete with developed regions in attracting the three types of foreign-funded enterprises. Our colleagues in Pingnan County say others have "3+1 industries,"[2] while they only have "3+1 roadblocks." With poor transportation, the path to riches becomes deadlocked. Therefore, our thinking is that we must throw our doors wide open and actively create the conditions to attract foreign investment. We should act as the local conditions allow – open up more in coastal counties with good conditions and not try to force the matter in mountainous counties with poor conditions. We advocate real results rather than phony achievements, and we don't want to open up just to say we did it.

We will develop the three types of foreign-funded enterprises according to our abilities, working on trade with Taiwan, using traditional ports and major coastal towns to develop trade, and working hard to create our own features in opening up to the outside world. As of now, there are more than 50 foreign-funded enterprises in our prefecture. This year we have already completed negotiations on foreign investment projects totaling more than 10 million US dollars. Nevertheless, the work we are doing now can only be chalked up as training for opening up, cultivating awareness, and laying the foundation for future development.

Notes

[1] This refers to the primitive construction of the roads.

[2] This refers to industries that process imported materials, process materials according to imported samples, assemble imported parts, and engage in compensatory trade. This form of international trade was developed as a business model in the beginning of the reform and opening-up period.

Thoughts on Economic Development in Ningde Prefecture

January 1989

Reporter: I have heard that in the six months since you came to Ningde from Xiamen you have gone to the grassroots to learn about the situation and you already have a deep understanding of the region. I have also heard that you place more emphasis on agriculture. Can you talk a little about this?

Xi Jinping: We can say that economic development in Ningde revolves around farmers to a large extent. Farmers account for the vast majority of the population – this is a basic fact in the region. Agriculture is a characteristic and also an advantage of Ningde. Of course, the agriculture we are talking about is not a small-farming economy, but rather "big agriculture" in the sense of the commodity economy. In the past few years, the economic power of Ningde has greatly increased, and an important manifestation of this is the sustained, steady development of agricultural production and its diversification.

Reporter: I heard you talk about the concept of "big agriculture," which includes your thoughts on industry. Can you talk about this in detail?

Xi Jinping: The idea of "big agriculture" is inseparable from using industry to supplement and facilitate agriculture. First, without a certain industrial foundation, we will have no financial power to speak of,

---

This is an interview with a reporter from *Fujian Tribune*, first published in *Fujian Tribune*, Issue No. 3, 1989.

and more investment in agriculture would be difficult. Next comes the reasonable adjustment of the internal structure of agriculture, as the formation of an agricultural and side-line product market requires industry as a catalyst. Of course, industry in Ningde should follow its own path. That means we must properly manage the relationship between resource development and industrial structure, focus on the processing and use of local resources, and develop industries with marketable products and local production advantages. The future of industrial development in Ningde lies in building a stable foundation for raw material supply, and we can't "cook a meal without rice."

Reporter: When we say that industry in impoverished regions cannot "cook a meal without rice," three popular topics in Ningde come to mind: developing the Sandu'ao port, building the Fuzhou-Wenzhou railway, and building a central city. May I ask your view on this?

Xi Jinping: I think it's good that people are talking about these three things. This shows that the people of Ningde have a better understanding of our natural environment. Of course, certain objective conditions need to be met before we can build upon what nature has already provided us with. Development projects such as ports and railways depend on macro state policies, and the formation of a central city is the result of long-term economic development. Ningde has unbalanced revenues and expenditures, and it will be difficult to try to undertake large-scale projects on our own at the moment. As the saying goes, "you cannot fly high without a full set of feathers."[1] We need to let more people outside of our region understand the significance of these three things, but we cannot base our future on this alone. Even though these things are possible and greatly needed, this does not mean they are going to happen. Decisions on the overall strategy for prefectural development must fully consider the national, provincial, and prefectural situations, and we cannot try to force the early realization of development goals that are unrealistic to achieve in the near future. What we must do now is focus on medium- and short-term work.

Reporter: What are your thoughts on rectifying the economic environment?

Xi Jinping: Rectifying the economic environment actually provides Ningde with an opportunity. The intentions of the central government (which is not to press hard on the brakes as some people mistakenly believe) are beneficial to developing the productive forces in regions that are economically backward. Ningde cannot afford to make unrealistic comparisons with others in terms of economic speed and size. The direction the central government is taking us in will allow Ningde to play to its advantages and make up for its shortcomings. We can use the opportunity of rectification to allow our region to realize stable, coordinated economic development. It just so happens that the central government's guidance to support agriculture, energy, transportation, communications, science and technology, education, daily necessities, and raw material industries covers the weak links in Ningde, and these are the areas we need to work on the most. We can use this opportunity of rectification to further optimize and integrate key production factors and reasonably adjust industrial structure.

Reporter: Coming from an opening-up region like Xiamen, what do you think an impoverished region like Ningde can learn from Xiamen when it comes to opening up to the outside?

Xi Jinping: The degree of opening up in one location is determined by the quality of its soft and hard environments. The practice of opening up in many locations the past few years has proven that tax exemptions and deductions are not as attractive as we thought, as foreign companies not only want to save money, they also want to make more money and be able to do business easily and smoothly. Ningde Prefecture can make great strides in building its soft environment, as simplifying procedures, lowering fees, increasing efficiency, and improving service will be very attractive to businesses. Ningde and Xiapu, the counties slated to be first to open up, should become the prefecture's trial zones for opening up to the outside world. I have especially noticed that it is critical to have an open mind. At the same time, we must avoid the "Matthew Effect" while opening up. If we don't handle it correctly, opening-up regions will become increasingly opening up, and closed regions will become increasingly closed, because there are conditions for opening up, while impoverished regions lack such conditions. Therefore, to prevent the "Matthew Effect," we must work hard to improve the conditions of impoverished regions. Building a good soft environment in impoverished regions will create conditions there for opening up. Compared to other regions, the officials and people in impoverished regions must feel greater urgency for building a sound soft environment, and I have no doubt they'll work very hard at this and accumulate good experiences in building a soft environment. This is almost the only path for impoverished regions to create conditions for opening up, and it is also a powerful assurance that impoverished regions will not fall behind when opening up is going on all around them. Of course, we must prevent the "Matthew Effect" from occurring in impoverished regions.

Reporter: Economic development requires clean governance, and clean governance in local authorities and departments boils down to the integrity of Party and government officials. What are your thoughts on this?

Xi Jinping: Integrity in Party and government organs bears on the survival of the Party and whether it will continue to win the support of the people, as well as the fate of the socialist economy. Now the people are calling loudly for clean government. There are four phrases that I think can serve as a wake-up call. The first is, "if a thing doesn't belong to us, we don't dare take a hair of it."[2] To me, this is a basic requirement for Party members and officials. The second phrase is, "you cannot get everything you want."[3] We cannot think we can serve as officials and also strike it rich. Public officials cannot covet wealth – this is a fast and true rule no matter where you are, regardless of the time. The president of the United States has an income far less than that of many prominent businesspeople; wealthy workers, farmers, and self-employed individuals will certainly have higher incomes than any of our officials. Any pursuit requires some sacrifice. The third phrase is, "with a clean conscience, all things become clear."[4] Party discipline and national laws do not allow for any corruption or exploitation of the people. The fourth phrase is, "working for the interests of the local people with each term in office."[5] The purpose of being an official is to contribute. And when it comes to profiting, we cannot "take it as our own" or covet material benefit and scheme for private gain.

Notes

[1] See "Intrigues of Qin (I)," in *Intrigues of the Warring States. Intrigues of the Warring States* is a compilation of anecdotes about strategies and speeches given by visiting scholars during the Warring States Period.

[2] See Su Shi, "Two Prose Poems on the Red Cliff." [Source of English translation: Su Shi, "Two Prose Poems on the Red Cliff," in *Selected Poems of Su Tung-p'o*, trans. Burton Watson (Port Townsend: Copper Canyon Press, 1994), 96. – *Tr.*]

[3] This is based on the following line from "Book 6A" of the *Mencius*, "I desire fish, and I also desire bear's paws. If I cannot have both of them, I will give up fish and take bear's paws." [Source of English translation: Mencius, "Book 6A," in *Mencius,* trans. Irene Bloom (New York: Columbia University Press, 2009), 127. – *Tr.*]

[4] See Anonymous (from the Song Dynasty), *Collection of Writings of Famous Worthies.*

[5] This is a line from Huang Zongxi (1610-1695). A native of Yuyao, Zhejiang Province, Huang Zongxi was a thinker and historian of the late Ming and early Qing dynasties.

Work for the Interests of the Local People with Each Term in Office

January 1989

Bridges and paths

The main responsibility of leaders is to resolve problems of "bridges" and "paths."

The "bridges" refer to building bridges that serve as channels for the people to develop commodity production. For example, leaders should make reasonable arrangements for the regional economy and provide correct guidance and effective services. This is not enough, however, as we must also focus on clearing some of the misconceptions among the people that arise from reform and opening up and straightening out certain relationships. For example, the Third Plenary Session of the 13th CPC Central Committee proposed the principle of "rectification and correction," and many people believe that this is a sign of slowing down or bringing to a halt of construction and reform. This is caused by people not understanding the spirit of the Third Plenary Session from a positive angle. Just as improving traffic order and repairing road surfaces are meant to let vehicles pass through more quickly, rectification is meant to create the necessary conditions for furthering reform. This demands that we both look to the big picture and take the local situation into consideration. We can

This is a conversation with a reporter from *Anhui Daily*, first published in *Anhui Daily* on January 18, 1989.

neither say we are exempt from following the Party Central Committee's principles due to our special circumstances, nor expect "rigid uniformity." Therefore, we should clean up disorder where it appears, never let the economy get too hot or too cold, protect or apply pressure when necessary, and facilitate and control where appropriate. All of this is part of the effort to drive healthy, stable economic development. This is what we mean by resolving problems of "bridges."

"Paths" refer to determining the path of local economic development, which must be done in light of the overall plans of the central and provincial authorities while considering the greater background and prerequisites of the entire task at hand and the actual local situation. Ningde Prefecture is an old revolutionary base area inhabited mostly by minorities; it is a remote, and impoverished mountainous region with 913 kilometers of coastline and over 300 islands. For readily apparent reasons, after the People's Republic was founded little investment has been made in this region, and its economy is still quite backward even today. What can we do? We must start from the actual situation and take advantage of the prefecture's geographical location. We must seize the opportunity to plan and implement a strategy for coastal economic development. We must not make unrealistic comparisons, sit on our hands, or act rashly. The key is in thriving through constraint and eventually realizing development. "A journey of a thousand miles starts from beneath one's feet."[1] Our first step must be to make sure we do what we can in the short term. This is the path we must follow.

Positive actions

Karl Marx once said, "Every step of real movement is more important than a dozen programmes."[2] I'm not calling for more slogans, but for positive actions. In the past we adopted many effective measures, and just like in a relay race the baton was passed forward, and with feet planted firmly on the ground real results were achieved.

In the past Ningde relied on agriculture, and in future we must still rely on the overall development of agriculture. Developing "big agriculture" is an unchangeable goal for Ningde and the basis for its farmers moving up from poverty to prosperity. In late 1985, the Fujian Provincial CPC Committee proposed "resolving food and clothing issues within three years" for the province's impoverished regions. The Prefectural Party Committee learned from the lessons of the poor results of "free loans to fight poverty" and "rallying thousands of troops to help thousands of families" programs, and adopted comprehensive measures such as joint efforts through-out society and establishing economic entities. After three years of support, the prefecture's poverty alleviation rate reached 87.3%, and some people were already on the road to prosperity. This was the right thing to focus on and the right thing to do, so we've decided to keep doing it for two more years without changing our policies. We'll focus on the key points, bring our work to new levels, increase the poverty alleviation standards, and strengthen the staying power of poverty alleviation. Specific measures will focus both on poverty alleviation for families and on development of township enterprises, bolstering the power of the collective economy at the township and village levels, and aiming to have ten model townships and towns that generate RMB100 million each in revenue. With a clear path laid out, the key to the next step lies in fighting easygoing pastoral sentiments and bad habits of overstaffing and lack of discipline, and promoting a work manner of taking on a full load and having high urgency and efficiency in which today's work gets finished today. I am all for daring to blaze new trails, daring to take certain risks, not simply follow-ing in the footsteps of others, and establishing a tradition in Ningde of "feeling no shame with our predicament, working with iron will, pressing boldly forward, and striving for excellence."

Governing with integrity

With clear work principles and policies, if we don't have good work manners and methods, it will be difficult for the principles and policies to play their anticipated role. I heartily embrace the Party Central Committee's judgment that "maintaining integrity in Party and government authorities directly bears on the survival of the Party and winning popular support." The purpose of being a Communist Party member is to forever serve the people. Therefore, the purpose of officials is to contribute, to serve, to be rooted in ideals, and to not simply seek to benefit oneself. "If a thing doesn't belong to us, we don't take a hair of it"[3] – this is a minimal requirement for Party and government officials. We despise those who use their own power to seek personal gain, who are corrupt and accept bribes, and who throw their weight around. Of course, governing with integrity itself is not enough. We must make achievements, be able to improve the local situation, advance economic development, and raise the people's standard of living. This is why I say government officials should "work for the interests of the local people with each term in office."

Notes

[1] See chapter 64 of *Dao De Jing*. [Source of English translation: Lao Zi, *Tao Te Ching*, trans. D.C. Lau (Harmondsworth: Penguin Books Ltd., 1972), 125. – *Tr.*]

[2] Source of English translation: Karl Marx, "Letter from Marx to Wilhelm Bracke," in *Karl Marx, Fredrick Engels: Collected Works*, vol. 45 (New York: International Publishers, 1991), 70. – *Tr.*

[3] See Su Shi, "Two Prose Poems on the Red Cliff." [Source of English translation: Su Shi, "Two Prose Poems on the Red Cliff," in *Selected Poems of Su Tung-p'o*, trans. Burton Watson (Port Townsend: Copper Canyon Press, 1994), 96. – *Tr.*]

Journalism: Mastering the Fundamentals

May 1989

Make objective analysis and get a clear understanding of the situation

The Party needs to exercise greater leadership in the field of journalism. Our attempts to better understand the profession and improve leadership should be integrated with the current situation. Journalism must have its finger on the pulse of the times. It must recognize the tasks and responsibilities that the current state of affairs thrusts upon it. Ten years of reform has brought great success, but there are still many trials ahead. It is not acceptable for journalists to stick to outdated methods, ignore reforms, or refuse to heed opinions that are raised. They should not simply parrot the words of others, jump on ideological trends, or report without boundaries. Otherwise, things will become muddled. When considering ideological trends in our society, we should stay cool and think by ourselves, without being at the mercy of our whims. Objective analysis takes time. Rushing to judgement frequently leads to one-sided, perhaps even faulty conclusions. Some current issues have made evident that our democratic process and legal system need to develop at a faster rate. We should establish specific, rational steps to determine how to increase that rate and what that rate should be. If we think of democracy in terms of

In mid-May 1989, political turmoil was fermenting in Beijing. Ningde Prefecture held a meeting concerning the work of the media and the fundamentals that journalists should address. At the meeting I talked about the topic. Xu Yiming, a Xinhua news reporter, recorded my views and had them published in *Chinese Journalists*, Issue No. 6, 1989.

absolutes, attempt to apply an advanced form of democracy in a society that is still maturing, or skip certain stages of development, then once reasonable demands may turn into serious blunders.

What is democracy? We should avoid painting it with a broad brush. My understanding is that democracy in a socialist country is manifested in a legal system that promotes the people's interests. Democracy should neither cater to the whims of specific groups or social strata, nor meet their demands. Those who go to extremes to place demands on the people and the country are really just insisting that they receive democratic treatment, with no restrictions on what they do or say and carrying no responsibilities to the government or other people. Does that sound right?! Would you accept this behavior or agree if everyone demanded to enjoy this kind of democracy?! Of course not. By allowing a specific person or people to enjoy this kind of democracy, not only do you lose your democratic rights, you deprive others of theirs.

Imagine if people did as they pleased. Family planning is ignored, taxes are not paid, and the army and police are disbanded. Finally, the prisons are opened up, and the inmates released. Work standards go out the window. Life no longer has any restrictions. Would you still feel confident about your democratic rights or your safety? Does this sound like a good idea? Real democracy does not come in the form of absolutes. It is subject to specific constraints. At the same time, democracy develops in stages and cannot be rushed. The way we cultivate the quality and management of our democracy must also follow specific stages. Let's take a look at our democracy as it stands now. Has it developed enough to be effective? How has it been applied in elections for village committees? Well, some places have done a good job. Villagers realized they needed to pick good leaders who would serve their fundamental interests. Other places elected clan elders or people willing to compromise their principles in order to get along with everyone else. This has paralyzed rural grassroots organizations. Therefore, when raising a question, we must keep in mind its basic premise and specific background and conditions. Otherwise, it is not possible to ask and answer a question effectively. After all, wasn't the Cultural Revolution[1] a prime example of "great democracy?" Instead of being integrated with science and the legal system, it was mired in superstition and ignorance. This "great democracy" led to great turmoil. Anyone can get a few people together to raid a home or pull together a fighting force. You knock me down today. I knock you down tomorrow. Does anyone want a repeat of this history? Without stability and unity, nothing else matters! Hence, the issue of democracy should be addressed within the legal system.

Then, there is the issue of corruption. This really stirs up our moral indignation. Whenever corruption rears its head, the outrage of honest journalists, and anyone who has a conscience, becomes palpable. Nevertheless, we cannot let emotions get the best of us when dealing with corruption. Moral indignation is not enough. We need to have practical ways of fighting corruption at our disposal. There are people who assail against corruption despite being the beneficiaries of special privileges. From birth to death, every stage of life presents opportunities to cut deals or engage in unhealthy tendencies. Neither a stethoscope nor a steering wheel confers power, but some doctors and drivers take advantage of their positions to make dishonest money. This is a phenomenon that calls for our reflection. We should ask why, get to its root causes, and then develop some solutions. Otherwise, we are looking at the phenomenon too simply.

Journalists need to keep up with the times and understand the true function of journalism. Charged with the important task of reporting and guiding public opinion, they should recognize the role of journalism as the voice of the Party and the people. Our Party has a tradition of using the newspaper, radio, and television to publicize the Party's guideline, principles, and policies. This is a way to educate the people and allow their voices to be heard. It helps develop healthy tendencies, expose corruption and other misconducts, and mobilize the people to participate in building socialism. Our Party places great importance on the deep affinity we share with the people. Ours is the Party that represents the people's interests. We have no interests of our own that are independent of the people's interests. We represent their immediate and long-term interests, as well as their local and general interests. I want to be clear that the Party's guideline, principles, policies, and positions fully reflect the wishes and demands of the people. Relatively speaking, people easily recognize when their immediate or local demands are met. They easily connect the Party's views and positions with events that occur around them. Recognizing their long-term or general interests is more difficult, as those who are in a given locality may not be fully aware of the general state of affairs due to individual differences in education, level of awareness, employment, regional geography, age, and other factors. After all, "Orchid and chrysanthemum flower at different times."[2] Not having the full picture may create distance and discrepancies between their views and those of the Party. In my opinion, journalists should focus more on serving as channels and bridges for communication. They should dedicate whatever time and patience is needed to inform the people about the Party's guideline, principles, and policies. Explaining the Party's positions and views will enable the people to have a better understanding of important events in the Party and the country. Equipped with this understanding, the people will naturally embrace the Party's positions and act accordingly.

Journalism is a science with close links to politics. That being said, I am not equating journalism with politics, or condoning the abandonment of journalistic truth for the sake of political necessity. Instead, I am encouraging the media to be more invested in the Party spirit as they uphold their journalistic standards.

Now is a critical time for the country's reforms. People's thoughts and sentiments vary greatly, and friction of interests among social groups occurs frequently. How do we settle these issues? It is imperative that we bring into full play the role of the media in publicizing the reforms and the Party's policies. The reforms are a great social practice. In order to ensure they remain on track and develop properly, the media need to communicate the principles and policies of our Party and government with accuracy and timeliness, report on the course of their implementation, and urge all levels of Party organizations and the government to promptly correct any errors. When confusion exists about certain issues, the media should provide guidance to clear up any contradictions. They should promote communication among the Party, the government, and the people, and try to bring different sides together. The media should also direct their efforts toward enhancing people's understanding and support of reforms, encouraging them to think and act in accordance with "one central task, two basic points,"[3] and guiding them to realize the Four Modernizations[4] and revitalize our economy and society. I commend journalists for the great contributions they have made to the success of reform and opening up over the past decade. They have worked hard. Journalists play a key role in establishing the Party's political advantage. The ability to promote our work through journalism demonstrates leadership and a modern way of work. Relations between leaders and the people can be categorized into the mystical and the open. Mystical relations are often associated with feudal, closed, or backward societies. Leaders who have open relations with the people tend to be in societies that are progressive and culturally advanced. Party committees at all levels in our prefecture must attach importance to the role of the media and strengthen their leadership of it.

Guide public opinion and foster healthy tendencies

Guiding public opinion and playing a watchdog role are two major functions of socialist journalism. Guiding public opinion refers to using news reports to foster healthy social tendencies. When I say "foster healthy tendencies," I mean guiding public opinion to shore up people's confidence in reforms, tell people about the bright future reforms will bring, and encourage people to adhere to the Four Cardinal Principles. In particular, we want to encourage everyone to follow the guiding principles of the central authorities, participate in rectification and correction, uphold the authority of the Party Central Committee and the State Council, and maintain political stability and unity. How can we be sure to guide public opinion in a way that "fosters healthy tendencies?" Well, it requires that all journalists emphasize positive publicity and master the fundamentals of news reporting. In previous years, there was a saying among the media people that "achievements won't evaporate even when nobody talks about them." Clearly, this idea does not present the full story. We have achieved a great deal over the past decade of reform. This constitutes the main part of our work, and our success has been recognized worldwide. Publicizing the news requires a down-to-earth approach in which journalists report on our achievements with confidence, helping to make the Party more cohesive and enhance government authority. These are important points for journalists to keep in mind. They need to grasp the essence of things, report on the dominant trend of issues, and take on the role of fostering healthy tendencies. When reporting on difficult issues or hot-button topics that attract great interest, the media should explain the nature of these issues to the public within the context of the achievements brought about by ten years of reform. The media should guide the public to help them understand that these issues are occurring during the period of cross-over in which the old system is being replaced by a new one and there are deficiencies in our democracy and legal system. In time, these issues will be reduced or eliminated completely with further reforms, socialist intellectual and cultural progress, and the development of democracy and rule of law.

While improving their guidance of public opinion, journalists also need to exercise their role as watchdog. This role is vital to the building of the Party and democratic politics. Corruption is inevitable when those in power are not subject to constraints or supervision. Whether we can curb corruption concerns the survival of our Party and the success of our socialist cause. Curbing corruption requires establishing a variety of monitoring mechanisms. The media's role as watchdog is the most open, extensive, and predominant way to monitor those in power. When emphasizing the building of the Party and the fight against corruption, it is crucial that we help the media exercise their role as watchdog so that corruption can be exposed. The government and Party organizations should encourage journalists to report on the bad as well as the good. We should wield this weapon of supervision to expose various forms of corruption and criticize problems that exist in our work. Leaders at all levels of the Party and government should approach the media's role as watchdog with the proper attitude. We need to be open-minded and refrain from demanding perfection of the media. We should befriend journalists, value their support for the work we do at the local level through their role as watchdog, and create a favorable political environment for their work.

When the media's watchdog role is used as a weapon, it must be wielded with a strong sense of social responsibility and an understanding of the effects it will have on society. It should be used to promote a political environment that is stable and unified, encourage reform and opening up, and help the Party carry out its work. The media should take an active and constructive role in monitoring the Party and the government. They should focus on gross violations of Party and government policies, and major issues that affect society. They can maximize their efforts by highlighting the most representative cases. Journalists should expose the facts and strive for accuracy. They should adopt a cautious approach when leveling criticism against Party committees and government, and guard against first impressions that may cloud their judgment. Journalists should conduct in-depth investigations and listen to multiple parties in order to draw conclusions that tally with the facts. However, it is important that the media refrain from directing criticism at those issues that are difficult to resolve in the short-term due to current limitations. Instead, journalists should inform the people about steps the Party and government are taking to overcome difficulties and resolve issues.

Enhance the ranks of journalists

Journalists should have a strong sense of social responsibility. We should be clear that news agencies and journalists work for the Party and the people. Regardless of time or place, they have a duty to the Party, the people, and the undertakings of reform and opening up. They need to remember the media's effect on the general public and learn to overcome one-sided reporting.

To perform their job well and write solid reports, journalists need to be earnest learners and have a deeper understanding of policies and theories. The development of the commodity economy has created a more colorful world that demands the media to have enough discernment to see past the surface and get to the heart of matters. This can only be done when journalists are well versed in policies and theories, knowledgeable about the law, and familiar with the rules of the commodity economy. This requires that every journalist is a person of principle who is capable of rational analysis. In short, journalists need to demonstrate a higher political caliber and a stronger knowledge base.

Continuing to work diligently in spite of difficulties must become second nature to journalists. They should uphold the Party's traditions of going deep into the realities of life and conducting investigations and research. The quality of their writing depends on their ability to delve into social realities and carry out thorough interviews. Some journalists in our region have been producing slipshod work. Lounging in their offices thinking up ideas, they base their reporting on information from bulletins or meetings. On the occasional trip to the countryside, they never do more than skimming the surface of things. A survey of news reports on the radio and in the newspaper makes it clear that very few offer quality in-depth reporting. There are a multitude of good stories that never see the light of day because journalists do not put enough effort into exploring social realities. Knowing how to investigate and do research is a basic skill and path to success for journalists. Only by exercising this basic skill will journalists develop into competent professionals who think in the correct way and do solid work.

Journalists should be self-disciplined and adhere to professional ethics. Yet we know that the practice of "buying" journalists is not unheard of in some places. This is entirely incompatible with their code of professional ethics. While only a minority engages in this type of behavior, it erodes the trust and respect that people have for the profession. Journalists are charged with the sacred duty of informing and educating the people. Those who want to educate others must first be educated themselves. They must be disciplined, honest, and fair. Whether it is political integrity or professional ethics, journalists must hold themselves up to a higher standard. Journalism is a noble profession. It demands that journalists conduct themselves with dignity, have a sense of self-respect, and always strive to do better. It is my hope that journalists will improve their professional standards and develop a good work manner.

Notes

[1] This refers to a political movement that was mistakenly initiated by Mao Zedong in May 1966 and ended in October 1976. Large segments of the population were drawn into the movement, which was exploited by the Lin Biao-Jiang Qing clique. It brought severe devastation to the Communist Party of China, the state, and the people.

[2] Source of English translation: Lu Xun (1881-1936), "An Impromptu," in *Lu Xun: Selected Poems,* W. J. F. Jenner (Beijing: Foreign Language Press, 1982), 55. – *Tr.*

[3] "One central task, two basic points" are the basis of the Party line to guide policymaking during the primary stage of socialism. "One central task" refers to economic development; "two basic points" refer to the Four Cardinal Principles and the reform and opening-up policy.

[4] This refers to the modernization of industry, agriculture, national defense, and science and technology.

Correctly Manage Six Relationships in Ningde's Economic Development

February 1989

Many factors have contributed to poverty in Ningde Prefecture, and it is our main duty to bring the region out of poverty toward prosperity. The coastal geographic environment, easing of cross-Strait relations, and adopting of the opening-up policy have brought new challenges to Ningde in implementing a coastal development strategy. The dual task of poverty alleviation and coastal development strategy has made the work in Ningde more significant and more difficult.

Since the Third Plenary Session of the 11th CPC Central Committee, there have been huge changes in Ningde's economy. Such changes are not dazzling short-term changes, but rather changes that have taken place gradually and accumulatively thanks to the determined efforts of all the people in the region. Such changes are a transition from quantity to quality and have the effect of water droplets drilling through rock. Future development in Ningde not only requires the spirit of arduous struggle, but also requires finding the path of economic development that most suits Ningde. I call the guiding thoughts behind this "methods that suit the location, categorized guidance, acting within our means, sparing no effort, and focusing on the benefits." To follow these guidelines we must properly manage six relationships in the economic development of Ningde.

Originally published in *Fujian Tribune*, May 1989.

1. The relationship between long-term objectives and short-term planning

Economic development requires a combination of long-term objectives and short-term planning. But while managing this relationship, it is tempting to seek quick results in economically underdeveloped regions. If we only pay our attention to projects whose conditions for accomplishment are not available in the short term and overlook the importance of timing and proper steps, then we will lose all short-, medium-, and long-term objectives. When I started working in Ningde last year, I frequently heard three topics of discussion: develop Sandu'ao, construct the Fuzhou-Wenzhou railway, and build a central city. The fact that people all over this region were discussing these topics shows, in my opinion, their strong desire for change and increased ability to recognize the issues. I have tried to lower people's expectations toward these three things because I want to emphasize the relationship between long-term objectives and short-term planning entailed in them. In the "Preface to *A Contribution to the Critique of Political Economy*," Karl Marx said, "Mankind thus inevitably sets itself only such tasks as it is able to solve, since closer examination will always show that the problem itself arises only when the material conditions for its solution are already present or at least in the course of formation."[1] Major development projects such as port and railway construction that can easily involve hundreds of millions of yuan in investments rely on macro policies at the national level. The formation of central cities is the result of long-term economic development. Ningde runs a large deficit, which makes it difficult for us to undertake such projects that require enormous investment on our own. This year and next, the country will be focusing on rectification, which means credit and money will be tight, and large-scale investment in Ningde will be impossible. Therefore, the right attitude should be to recognize the three main objectives and actively publicize and make preparations for them. We must study future development strategies, but they should be based on a profound understanding of the situation at the prefectural, provincial, and national levels, and we should use this understanding to formulate an "ambitious overall strategy." We should only look to carry out work that is feasible, and our long-term objectives must be gradually realized in concrete steps. We must both avoid pushing for unrealistic early achievement of long-term objectives and prevent oversimplification of short-term planning.

2. The relationship between the rate of economic development and economic benefits

Speed and benefits are opposing goals that are difficult to reconcile, and it is hard to find the right midpoint between the two. I believe that we should try to coordinate speed of development and economic benefit in order to gain greater benefits. "Try to hurry, and you accomplish nothing."[2] We should see that pursuit of high speed often excessively squeezes resources, giving the overall economy no room to breathe, and excessive speed has a destructive effect on the development of the productive forces. We stress putting economic benefits first for two reasons: to check inappropriate speed of economic development, and to take into consideration the realities of Ningde. This region has weak foundations and cannot take excessive strain, and we must make sure projects of hundreds of thousands of yuan and above will be successful. Ningde has limited investment channels, so we must pay attention to steering investment toward projects that deliver benefits. Ningde has low levels of management skills, and its product profit margin and contribution to tax revenue are below provincial averages. Currently one-third of its production capacity is not up to full speed. Therefore, there is still ample room for greater benefits through increasing production quality and efficiency and tapping new potential. On the other hand, we should see that even though Ningde has made great achievements these past few years, its main economic indicators are still falling proportionally when we look at the entire province. Therefore, suitable development speed is still necessary. This can keep us from falling further behind in the entire province and the country at large, and prevent inaction and failure to pursue development.

3. The relationship between resource development and adjustment of industrial structure

There are two prerequisites to properly managing this relationship: first, Ningde is rich in resources, but the development and use of these resources are determined by having reasonable industrial policies; second, adjustment of the industrial structure in Ningde should be made primarily in light of the current state of local resources. The resources of Ningde are distributed unevenly, but the distribution of industries in the region is more or less even. In other words, the industrial structure does not match the resources, and there are no clearly dominant industries. Leaders at all levels should pay close attention to the mismatch between resource distribution and industrial structure.

For regional economic development in both developed countries and developing countries, if the appropriate industrial policies are not in place, structural productive forces cannot be fully released, and economic growth will not have the speed and benefits that it should realize. Therefore, Ningde should formulate regional industrial policies to determine the optimal structure, priority, and timing of industrial development.

Ningde has excellent potential for its agricultural, forestry, and hydropower resources. I believe that this kind of regional situation should be the basis for adjusting industrial structure in Ningde. Agriculture is an advantage of the region. In the past, development relied on agriculture. Going forward, we still will rely on comprehensive development of agriculture. But we must go beyond traditional farming under the constraints of the natural economy, and step up to "big agriculture" in the comprehensive commodity economy.

Although Ningde has many mountains, the foundation for the forestry industry is poor. Our forest cover and reserves are low. We should adopt positive guiding principles and formulate policies that recognize the strategic role of forestry in poverty alleviation in the region. It is worth stressing that the edible mushroom industry has facilitated economic development in Ningde, but we must properly manage the relationship between this and other industries, in particular the forestry industry. Areas with rapid development in the edible mushroom industry can link forestry to mushrooms.

The all-round development and use of Ningde's sea-based resources are still in the initial stages. We should pay close attention to building pelagic sea fishing fleets. The depth and breadth of shallow sea and tidal land aquaculture should be increased. For shrimp farming, which has already seen some development, we should focus on increasing per-unit yield. For high-end fish, shellfish, and algae farming, we should expand the farming area. The hydropower industry is also a major resource advantage of Ningde. I advocate actively developing hydropower resources in Ningde according to our abilities. Hydropower is a basic industry and also one with good benefits, therefore "as soon as we have money, build power stations." We can raise funds for small power stations and seek to build medium-sized stations with foreign capital or through joint ventures. Gradually, we will form an electric power system in Ningde with hydropower as the dominant source, integrated with the provincial power grid to accommodate peak usage. We can also integrate factories into the power system to develop the metallurgy industry in Ningde.

I must emphasize that one of the most basic principles of industrial development in Ningde is that development should be compatible to the capacity for self-balancing. The adjustment of industrial structure in each county of Ningde can identify a leading industry or industry groups based on local resources and productive forces. Investment policies targeting leading industries can be formulated and implemented to expedite their development. In turn, growth in the leading industries will drive the development of upstream and downstream industries. For example, Gutian has the deep processing of mushrooms; Zherong has pharmaceuticals; Xiapu has massage tools and processing of seaweed, nori, and mustard root; and Fu'an has electrical machinery and ferroalloys. These are all promising industries. For these industries that have sufficient supplies of raw materials and ready markets, we should adopt powerful measures to grow them to achieve mass production and pursue the benefits of economies of scale.

Of course, the rules of economic development show us that continued industrial development will inevitably tilt the balance of local resources, and considerable raw materials from other places will be needed. However, industrial development should still be based on the processing and use of local resources.

4. The relationship between mountainous and coastal areas in the distribution of productive forces

The dual economic states of the coastal and mountainous areas constitute a special problem in the economic development of Ningde. To recognize the content and implications of this special problem we must consider it from different angles. First, from the viewpoint of historical materialism, people cannot freely choose their own forces of production, and all historical forces of production are the starting point for the productive lives of the next generation. Therefore, coastal and mountainous areas both have their own path of economic development to follow. Second, objectively, there are differences between the coastal and mountainous areas, and this makes it possible for them to engage in complementary cooperation. The economic development strategy of Ningde must consider how to coordinate such differences. Therefore, policy formulation cannot be rigidly uniform, and in implementation we should take into account the differences and cooperation between the coastal and mountainous regions.

The revitalization of the mountain economy and development of the coastal economy are both important to bringing the economy of Ningde to a new level. This does not mean, however, that we will implement a balanced strategy in handling these two types of economies as we address regional distribution of productive forces. I believe that the distribution of productive forces should be varied. That is, we should take the path of "unbalanced-balanced-unbalanced" distribution of productive forces based on the reality of unbalanced economic conditions. Taking investment as an example, we should use input-output coefficients to determine the quantity and direction of investment and implement targeted investment policies. The reasons for this are clear. First, investment is not "relief." We do not necessarily invest more in poorer areas. Second, within a certain period, returns from investment in more economically developed areas are greater and faster. Of course, this does not mean that there should be no investment in mountainous regions. I simply mean that there should be overall priorities, and the proportion of investment can be increased for specific investment projects in mountainous regions where the benefits will be good.

The coastal region, in particular the Fuzhou-Wenzhou highway belt, is where industry is more highly concentrated in Ningde. This region's industrial output accounts for more than 70% of the entire prefecture, and its fiscal revenue accounts for 64.8% of the entire prefecture. Fuding, Fu'an, and Xiapu counties each has industrial outputs of over 100 million yuan. This is a priority area in the distribution of our productive forces. We envision centering growth around Saiqi, extending growth to the inland from the Fuzhou-Wenzhou highway belt, and gradually advancing toward the mountainous regions.

5. The relationship between reform and opening up and poverty alleviation

I believe that for Ningde, the initial and ultimate purposes of opening up and poverty alleviation are both for the development of the commodity economy, so they should be aligned as they evolve, and the rules of commodity economy should apply to both. This "alignment theory" has three levels of significance. First, there is a certain difference between opening up and poverty alleviation. Specifically, they evolve in different forms and follow their own patterns, so we must have different policies and measures for the two areas of work. Second, opening up and poverty alleviation are interconnected. So we advocate approaching poverty alleviation with an open mind and leveraging opening-up policies in poverty alleviation. Third, opening up and poverty alleviation rely on each other to progress. Achievements from poverty alleviation serve as a new starting point for opening up, and opening up will bring poverty alleviation work to new levels. Therefore, we must strive to maximize overall performance and benefits. Based on the above understanding, both opening-up and poverty alleviation policies should play a role in developing the economy of Ningde, and the work in both areas should have its own characteristics.

The national government has listed Xiapu and Ningde counties of the prefecture as opening-up coastal counties. The counties that are not included in this list still face the question of how to open up, and people in these counties also need to have the notion of opening up on their mind. Ningde is exploring its way forward towards opening up, but there are four points that we should be clear about. First, we should not blindly follow the methods of the special economic zones and set up isolated development zones far from old urban centers. We must rely on our current cities – that is, we must build upon what we already have. Second, the practice of opening up over the past few years in a number of places has told us that tax exemptions and deductions are not the most important considerations for foreign investors. They aren't looking just to save money. They care more about making more money and making money easily. We can make Ningde more attractive to foreign businesses by improving our soft environment. For example, we can simplify procedures, lower fees, provide one-stop service for foreign investors, and prevent multiple departments acting on their own and frequently passing the buck. Third, we must coordinate foreign trade and across-the-Strait trade. As we vigorously develop the "3+1" industries and foreign trade, we should also expand trade with Taiwan and bring in new investment from Taiwan. Fourth, we must combine resource development and opening up, and leverage resources particular to Ningde to increase our attractiveness to the outside world.

Poverty alleviation work in Ningde has already made historic achievements, and 87.3% of impoverished households have their basic needs met in food and clothing. However, as opening up progresses, poverty alleviation work must be brought up to a new level. We must further the reform in Ningde. Every thing we do must be centered on reform, and poverty alleviation work must be carried out in the spirit of reform. Poverty alleviation funds should not be scattered about like pepper. Over 90% of poverty alleviation funds must be used to support economic entities at the county, township, and village levels in order to boost their vitality. We must give priority to supporting hundred-million-yuan towns and townships, model science and technology towns and townships, the Spark Program, non-staple food supply, and commodity bases for creating foreign exchange through exports. We must work hard to build small economic development zones and coordinate poverty alleviation with regional economic development. We must properly carry out two-step rural reform, improve the two-tiered responsibility system, further promote land operations at a suitable scale, and encourage farmers to increase investment in agriculture. A specialized and market-oriented service system for agricultural production must also be improved along with the comprehensive development of agriculture. Enterprise reform must introduce a competition mechanism on the basis of improving the contract system. We must optimize the organization of labor, strive to "arrive through one continual push," and boldly advance leasing and auction reforms. Where conditions are right, enterprises can also try out stock ownership systems. On the whole, the property rights relationship between the state and enterprises must be simplified; simple, non-paternal relations must be established through taxation; and conditions must be created for enterprises to compete in the market.

6. The relationship between science, technology, education
and economic development

For impoverished regions, we must emphasize the major role of science, technology and education (S & T education) in economic development. But due to the low level of economic development, S&T education faces insufficient funding, and problems have arisen. For example, should this sum be invested in education or in the factories?

Of course, an underdeveloped economy cannot be used as an excuse for not carrying out S&T education. On the contrary, it is precisely because the economy is underdeveloped that we must have all the more motivation and pressure to step up S&T education. S&T education and economic development have a mutually causal relationship, and we cannot wait until the economy has been developed to start our education. "It takes ten years to grow trees, but a hundred years to cultivate people." Delaying a few years means losing opportunities for a generation. The competing priorities of S&T education and economic development simply remind us that we must take note of three things. First, we must view S&T education from a long-term strategic perspective and see S&T education as a top-priority for economic and social development in Ningde. Second, with an underdeveloped economy, we must seek to get the most from S&T education. Third, we must convert progress in S&T education into kinetic energy that drives economic development, stressing both access and the "practical effect" of S&T education.

To every problem, there is a solution. For education, our principle is to pursue both "universal education" and "adult education." We must especially support vocational training and rural literacy work. All of society needs to do something for education, which is provided in various forms through multiple channels. We should strive to secure basic facilities[3] for elementary and higher-level schools by 1990. We should direct efforts to all types of training, such as practical rural technology training, and S&T and management training for officials and employees. S&T should be oriented toward production and rural realities, and S&T professionals should be encouraged to play a greater role in commodity production. We must also emphasize applied S&T, leverage S&T in the adjustment of urban and rural industrial structures, and promote the participation of S&T professionals in the Spark Program.

Notes

[1] Source of English translation: Karl Marx, "A Contribution to the Critique of Political Economy, Part One," in *Karl Marx, Fredrick Engels: Collected Works,* vol. 29 (New York: International Publishers, 1987), 263. – *Tr.*

[2] Source of English translation: Confucius, "Book Thirteen," in *The Analects of Confucius,* trans. Burton Watson (New York: Columbia University Press, 2007), 91. – *Tr.*

[3] This refers to classrooms that are equipped with chairs and desks, and housed in safe buildings.

Both Sides of Ningde's Fiscal Economy in the New Situation

March 1989

Now the economy is overheating and needs to cool off. To talk about fiscal issues at this time, I think we should focus more on talking about how to strengthen the regulating role of fiscal levers. Some may ask, in an impoverished region such as Ningde with flimsy fiscal power that is barely able to keep its head above water, what kind of a role can public finance play?

Some view public finance as a money purse. In this view, when we run out of money, the purse of course will be of little use. But this is an outdated notion, a simplified view of public finance that we criticized long ago. Public finance is so much more than simply managing a purse of revenues and expenditures. Rather, it is a giant lever that can be used to influence the economy. This should be self-apparent. Therefore, when we talk about applying fiscal levers, we cannot simply take it to mean giving more money to a certain location or collecting more money from another location. The effectiveness of the fiscal levers depends on the handling of several relations in public finance. To properly handle these relationships, we have to apply dialectical methods, which means using the views of dialectical materialism to study and resolve contradictions in the operation of Ningde's public finance.

1. Correctly handling the relationship between the overall and local situations

In public finance, the relationship between the overall and local situations is mainly a relationship between focus and coverage. Now the nation's finances face challenges, and all levels of sub-national governments are also in financial difficulties. Here in Ningde, our difficulties are even greater. In this situation, it is all the more necessary to properly handle the relationship between focus and coverage. Over the past few years we have had good coverage but lacked focus. The enthusiasm of local governments and enterprises for economic development has been mobilized, but macro-control has been weakened. This has led to an overheating economy and unmet demand for consumption. Therefore, we must emphasize the necessity to look at the big picture. The overall consideration for Ningde must be aligned with the overall consideration for the province and even the country. If we need to sacrifice local interests for the greater good as the nation rebalances the macroeconomy, we should do so willingly. Our impoverished region is in no place to talk about making contributions to national finances, but there is something we can do to help: we should not put our hand out to take money from the central coffer for unjustifiable reasons, and when we do have the need, we should try to not ask for more than what we truly need. Last year the entire prefecture implemented a fiscal budget management system in which "each level is responsible for itself and seeks out balance itself." In principle, governments at all levels should deal with their own deficits independently rather than hoping to rely on outside help.

2. Correctly handling the relationship between fiscal tightening and economic development

Fiscal tightening will be a basic national macroeconomic policy for the next few years. We must correctly and comprehensively understand this economic policy. Fundamentally speaking, the fiscal tightening we are talking about does not go against our goal of economic development. It is like taking one step back, then two steps forward. Or we can say that it is like crouching down while getting ready to make a great leap forward. Tightening does not mean blind tightening, but rather strictly applying controls where appropriate, resolutely eliminating where appropriate, and promoting growth where appropriate. This is called thriving through constraint and eventually realizing development. What we want to eliminate through tightening is behavior that disturbs socioeconomic order and violates the rules of economic operations. We should cut off all lifelines supporting such behavior. This kind of tightening is more beneficial to the healthy development of the economy.

Correctly handling the relationship between fiscal tightening and economic development requires astute assessment of the situation and decisive action when the time is right. First, the macro policy of fiscal tightening actually provides us with a good opportunity to optimize industrial structure and make reasonable use of resources. This is in line with the development strategy of Ningde. We certainly can concentrate our forces and strive to develop a range of "flagship" products claiming significant shares of the market and profitable enterprises that make major contributions to tax revenue. At the same time, we can gradually eliminate burdensome products and projects that hamper the growth of public revenue. Second, fiscal tightening may likely cause a short supply of capital to enterprises. This requires us to strengthen enterprise management, uncover potential sources of capital within enterprises, and grow businesses by enhancing production quality, efficiency and technological progress. If our enterprises can improve their management levels, they not only can survive in difficult circumstance, but they can also develop.

3. Correctly handling the relationship between increasing fiscal revenue and boosting enterprise vitality

When we mention boosting enterprise vitality, some colleagues call for "reducing profit turnover and taxes." When we mention increasing fiscal revenue, they think of "squeezing it out of enterprises." I think we cannot have this kind of understanding. Increasing fiscal revenue and boosting enterprise vitality should be two sides of the same coin rather than two distinct issues, as the two cannot be separated. To increase fiscal revenue, we need stronger and more sources of revenue. Where are these sources? They are mainly in enterprises. As enterprises thrive, revenue streams in, continually replenishing the public treasury. As the sayings go, a rising tide lifts all boats, and there is always enough water with a big enough spring. Therefore, from a fiscal perspective, we must enable enterprises to thrive. From the perspective of enterprises, the objective of running good business is to improve productivity and obtain good economic benefits. This actually opens up new sources of revenue. Therefore, boosting enterprise vitality and increasing fiscal revenue are essentially the same. Will there be conflicts? Of course. But these are conflicts within the system as a whole, mainly manifested in the balance between "give" and "take." Do we first give, then take, or vice versa? How much should we give, and how much should we take? When do we give, and what is a good time to take? If the government's finance and taxation departments are only there to take from enterprises, or enterprises only want more money from the government, what would the result be? The only result would be intensified conflicts. Let us share the correct approach. As we strengthen the state's ability to carry out macroeconomic regulation and control, any "take" must not negatively impact the enthusiasm, development, or legitimate rights and interests of the enterprises. In particular, increasing fiscal revenue must be in synch with boosting the vitality of large and medium state-owned enterprises that are important to the economy. We must take a forward-looking approach to public finance, in which we "first give to cultivate revenue sources and then take" and master the art of "you must first give to receive." We cannot act so foolishly as to catch the fish by draining the pond. In particular, under the current situation of fiscal tightening, fiscal departments must provide strong support for industrial and agricultural development through pumping up the flow of capital.

The economic relationship between public finance and enterprises is mainly reflected in taxes. To correctly handle the relationship between "give" and "take" at present, we must pay special attention to the problems of fiscal leaks and losses. Tax evasion is a fairly serious issue among sole proprietors, and we can also take a good look at the tax compliance situation among state-owned enterprises. Tax evasion is what I meant by fiscal leak. Fiscal losses mainly refer to mismanagement of "give" and "take." If tax reduction is not accompanied by effective management within an enterprise, the enterprise will not fully benefit from the "give," and the public treasury will not receive a return that is worth the "give." Going forward, our attention should be focused on supporting enterprise development and production through policies, work, and credit, and not on tax reduction. For enterprises that want to make their contribution to economic development, they can do so by strengthening management, improving profitability, and working hard to unlock their potential. This is especially true when state finances face difficulties.

4. Correctly handling the relationship between getting more done and acting within our means

The desire to do something for the people is a valuable one. Impoverished regions have poor foundations and await development in many areas. Many of our colleagues want to quickly move forward with work in their region and department, and this sentiment is understandable. But there is the problem of the reasonable use of financial resources. I believe that we can get more things done, but we must act within our means. These are two sides that must be balanced on the whole, and the dialectical relationship between the two in our work calls for our attention.

First, we must clearly assess the situation and make correct use of funds to do good work. When considering the amount of funding for non-production projects, we must not "take the food reserved for tomorrow and eat it today." That is, we cannot finance non-production projects with debt. No matter how good our intentions are, for non-production projects such as some building constructions, buying a moment's glory with borrowed money will only sow the seeds for future disaster. Of course, for production of projects, in particular production of products in short supply, we can take on a manageable debt. We should not shy away from funding production that has a far-reaching and positive impact on economic development simply because we do not have enough resources now. Playing safe in this regard would lose out on opportunities and our own future.

Second, we must economize and maximize the benefits in order to get more done. As we say, each penny helps, and every penny must be spent with care. This kind of practical spirit should be commended. To maximize the benefits means to use our limited financial resources on projects that are urgently needed for the national economy and society and produce quick results. When it comes to investment, we must consider the benefits. Investment should not be made where inappropriate or impossible. We should not invest today when an investment tomorrow will have the same result. More feasibility studies will help.

Third, when trying to get more done, we should seek real results and do what is urgently needed. To get real results, we must take concrete actions and strike a good balance between short-term and long-term interests. In our long-term strategy for development, we should engage in more cost-effective projects that deliver fast results. We cannot stop our projects halfway, get involved in "marathon" projects, or seek undeserved acclaim. When doing things that are urgently needed, we should keep sight of the big picture and prioritize. Public funding should be first provided to key projects that are urgently needed and have major significance for developing the national economy.

Opening Up the Economy of
the She People

April 1989

The She people are the largest minority ethnic group of Ningde. With a large She population residing all over the region, any effort to alleviate poverty in Ningde must take them into consideration. We should recognize that due to historical and geographical reasons, the economy of the She people has been constrained within a narrow regional circle. It has essentially remained barter-based, and any links with the outside economy are extremely frail. One key to developing the economy of the She people is in opening up, stepping out of their currently limited world. Human history has always been one of development through opening up. No ethnic group can develop solely by relying on their own power. History has shown us that development is only possible through open economic and cultural exchanges with the outside world.

Opening up requires first establishing the notion of a commodity economy. The economy of the She people requires help from outside to develop, but more importantly requires its own internal drive. Getting its internal drive started requires turning the old concept of isolation formed in a natural economy into new thinking that is needed to develop the socialist commodity economy.

The main goal for opening up the economy of the She people is to seek comprehensive development. The She areas have much potential in their resources, but potential does not equate to real economic power. We must develop the prefecture's natural resources to turn potential into real benefits. An important condition for resource development is market demand. When we talk about resource development, we mean comprehensive – rather than unbalanced – development that meets the needs of the socialist commodity market. It is part of all-round economic development. This kind of development does not simply look to economic benefits, but rather to overall benefits to society, the economy, and the environment.

Bringing life to commodity trading is a focus in the opening up of the economy of the She people. Some She areas have been closed off for a long time without much interaction with the outside world, and there are many detrimental factors affecting market development. In some places it is extremely difficult for the She people to engage in buying or selling. We must implement opening-up policies and break down the various barriers by introducing multiple types of economic entities, exchange channels, and operation methods to the She economy. Opening up the She economy requires a virtuous cycle where commodity trade drives commodity production, which in turn drives commodity trade. And I'm positive that such a cycle can be established.

Even though the economy of the She people of Ningde got off to a late start, is on a somewhat shaky foundation, and has more limiting factors, as long as it starts to open up, there is great hope for continued, stable development.

Forests Are the Key to Ningde's Revitalization

– Thoughts on a Strategic Issue for Economic Development in Ningde

January 1989

"Here there are rows of lofty mountains with lush forests and tall bamboos." In impoverished regions such as Ningde, mountain and forest resources are an important advantage. "When all the mountains of Ningde are green, Ningde will prosper." This popular saying among the people of this region reflects a profound truth: The potential for economic development in Ningde lies in the mountains, and its forests will make it thrive. What, then, is the correct understanding of this development strategy? I believe that in a general sense the forest industry brings great ecological and social benefits, such as beautifying the environment, replenishing water resources, conserving the soil, blocking wind and consolidating sand, regulating the climate, and creating virtuous cycles in the ecological environment. In particular, developing the forest industry is a main path Ningde can take to extricate itself from poverty and achieve prosperity. Forestry is one of the main sources of fiscal revenue in the region, and is a mainstay for developing local agriculture, industry, and township enterprises as well as a main foundation for foreign exchange earned through exports. It is also no exaggeration to say that forests also serve as water reservoirs, financial treasuries, and food granaries.

Since the Third Plenary Session of the 11th CPC Central

Committee, Ningde's forest industry has seen great development. Through measures such as planting, rebuilding, renewing, and intensive management, the entire region has built more than seven million *mu*[1] of forest mainly for timber production, but also for non-timber products, conservation, and firewood and charcoals. We have seen some promising initial results and have begun to reap the rewards of nature's favor. But we have far more to do. Based on a horizontal comparison and looking at long-term development, Ningde's forest industry still faces serious problems. Its forest coverage and green coverage are both below provincial-wide average levels. Despite much planting in recent years, there has been more logging, resulting in a "forest deficit" of 300,000 cubic meters. The prefecture also has more than 3.4 million *mu* of uncovered mountainous area and nearly 500,000 *mu* of sparse forests that can be rebuilt. We have many precious forest resources that have been left unused, and we still have not tapped our mountain-based resources.

As an old saying goes, we should be vigilant in times of peace. How much more vigilant we must be, given that today's reality does not allow us to have any "peace" of mind! We must truly make revitalizing the forest industry a strategic part of Ningde's economic development, take the initiative, and make no mistake about the urgency of the matter.

How can we seize the moment and bring the forest industry in Ningde to a new level? We must first have a set of clear guidelines: further reform the forestry system, fully mobilize all parties concerned, and strengthen the ability for self-development in forestry. Focusing on forests, we must strengthen management and protection, engage in three-dimensional development, speed up forest creation, and enhance the overall benefits of the forest industry. We will mobilize social forces to develop the forest industry, and closely link forestry development with food production, foreign exchange earnings through exports, poverty alleviation, and cultural progress.

Based on this set of guidelines, one basic requirement for Ningde in developing its forest industry is to focus on three key areas: awareness of the situation; fundraising from multiple sources; and implementation of management, protection, and development measures. Our other requirements are to resolve two tough problems: the forestry policy system, and ancestral rights to the mountains, so as to increase economic, social, and ecological benefits.

With the above guidelines and basic requirements, we can draw a blueprint for revitalizing Ningde's forest industry: work hard for seven years to ensure the target of covering all barren mountains with grass or trees by 1995: realizing prefecture-wide green coverage of 70% and forest coverage of 51%, an increase of 14 and 10.8 percentage points respectively – in order to reach or exceed provincial targets.

To achieve these goals, we must steadily and firmly grasp two segments: one is improving the responsibility system for the forest industry, and the other is building a robust forest management mechanism.

1. Improving the responsibility system for the forest industry

On the surface our prefecture's forest industry has completed its "three tasks,"[2] but actually the policies regarding the private-use of mountains and mountains managed under a responsibility system in some regions have not been implemented properly. People still worry about changes in the policies. In particular, "ancestral mountains" have restricted the development of the forest industry in many places. Now we must complete the "three tasks" and truly resolve the problem of "ancestral mountains." We must make a long-term commitment to affirming that "the ownership and benefits belong to the one who builds it," and to affirming the principle of allowing transfers. While keeping mountain rights unchanged, we should allow and encourage joint inter-regional development.

We must properly implement a goal-based responsibility system for the forest industry among leading officials. In the past two years, Gutian and Pingnan counties have had good results in implementing this system. We should spread their experience and implement this system throughout the prefecture at all levels. We should also combine it with the building of the "five main bases" (forest bases for timber production, oil production, quality product production, Moso bamboo production, and tea leaf production) and "two belts" (coastal protective forest belt and greening belt along the Fuzhou-Wenzhou highway) in our prefecture, which are two priorities for the prefecture this year. These will be used as the main indicators when we assess the performance of leading officials at the county, city, and township levels. Once the goal is set and promise made, officials must follow it through, and they will be rewarded for good performance and punished for poor performance.

2. Building a robust forest management mechanism

First, we must strictly prevent indiscriminate logging and step up the management and protection of resources. We must also thoroughly correct the past practice of "stressing planting but overlooking management, and logging excessively," which has led to a sharp drop in forest resources. This requires managing forests in accordance with the law, promptly investigating cases of forest destruction, prosecuting criminals who destroy forests, and establishing new order for production in forest areas. Towns and villages in forest regions must formulate local rules and regulations, get the people fully involved, and do more to prevent forest fires and control forest pests and diseases.

Second, we must move away from uniform operations and engage in comprehensive development. Industrial structure should be diverse to include forests, tea, fruit, and medicine. Maturity cycles should be a mix of "long, medium, and short terms." Land use should combine intercropping and free-range farming. Forest structure should integrate trees, shrubs, and grass. And finally, business management should seek to align economic, ecological, and social benefits.

Third, intensive management methods must be developed to replace crude methods. Forestation planning should turn from haphazard planting to targeted planting concentrated around select catchment areas and mountain ranges. Forestation investment should move away from the past thinly-spread "pepper shaker" method to focusing on forestation projects. In terms of forestation techniques, crude planting should be abandoned, and science and technology should be employed with a focus on the quality of planting. In terms of tree variety, the past uniform structure that mainly centered on firs and Chinese red pines should become diverse and dense with multiple layers, giving priority to trees of short maturity periods and high benefits. With reasonable arrangements, forestation planning, design, and implementation will see coordinated development throughout the prefecture.

Revitalizing Ningde through forestation is a hope-filled cause. All undertakings require arduous work to get started, and this is especially true in impoverished regions. As *Zuo's Chronicles*[3] profoundly puts it, it is like "heading off for the mountain forest in tattered clothing hauling a firewood cart."[4] Such a vivid image aptly depicts those who work hard to initiate a new undertaking in Ningde. I trust that as long as our officials and people share the same understanding and work together relentlessly for three, five, or even ten years, the forest industry in Ningde will see remarkable development, and there will be clear improvements in the prefecture's backward economy.

Notes

[1] One *mu* is equivalent to one-fifteenth of a hectare.

[2] The "three tasks" are to clarify the rights to forestland and mountainous areas, demarcate private land in mountainous areas, and establish a production responsibility system for the forest industry.

[3] Generally attributed to Zuo Qiuming, *Zuo's Chronicles*, also called *Zuo's Commentary on the Spring and Autumn Annals*, is considered part of the Confucian canon. Along with *Gongyang's* and *Guliang's*, it is one of the "Three Commentaries" that explain the *Spring and Autumn Annals*.

[4] See "The Twelfth Year of Duke Xuan," in *Zuo's Chronicles*.

Strengthening the Great Unity of All Ethnic Groups

– Reflections on Promoting the Common Prosperity of Ethnic Minorities

June 1989

Ningde Prefecture is inhabited by a large ethnic minority population. It is home to more than 100,000 members of the She ethnic minority, who make up 40% of the total She population throughout China, and 70% of the total She population in the province. These unique circumstances distinguish the work being done with ethnic minorities in Ningde. There are many facets to our work, but one that should never be underestimated is the handling of matters that involve ethnic minorities. This should serve as the guiding principle when we ponder how to promote the common prosperity of ethnic minorities. Our purpose is to strengthen the great unity of all ethnic groups.

1. Fully understand the historical and immediate significance of ethnic affairs and the unity of all ethnic groups

Issues that involve ethnic minorities are sensitive topics that can become quite complex. Ethnic groups are stable communities that have been formed over the course of history. This stability comes in part from the common psychology that people from a specific ethnic group share (including characteristics that are expressed in their culture and sentiments that are reflected in their collective self-consciousness). In the past, societies that oppressed ethnic minorities inhibited and destroyed their ethnic pride and sentiment. This did not change fundamentally until the socialist period, when all ethnic groups enjoyed comprehensive development and common prosperity, and when the pride and sentiment of all ethnic groups were recognized and allowed to develop. People of all ethnic groups cherish the stable socialist relations of equality, unity, and mutual assistance. The state has always taken issues that involve ethnic minorities very seriously. Ethnic minorities are also concerned about these sensitive issues, including the percentage of people with minority backgrounds who have been recruited for jobs or enrolled as students, and whether respect has been shown to the customs, practices, languages, and religious beliefs of ethnic minorities. The improper handling of issues such as these increases the possibility of social unrest or even political instability.

Mao Zedong said, "...the unity of our various ethnic groups, these are the basic guarantees for the sure triumph of our cause."[1] The history of Ningde has proven this point. During China's revolutionary war, the unity of all ethnic groups was crucial to stoking revolutionary fires throughout Ningde. It helped preserve and expand our forces during the most difficult years. Many veterans of the revolution were saved by the She people, who sacrificed their own blood, and even their own lives, to shield them. When veterans of the revolution such as Ye Fei[2], Zeng Zhi[3], and Fan Shiren[4] were engaged in guerrilla warfare in Fujian, they often sought shelter in She villages in the mountains. The revolutionary spirit of the She people is unshakeable. A veteran once told me that not one member of the She community of Ningde ever turned traitor during the war. That is quite extraordinary. During the socialist period, the She people, who are smart and industrious, once again contribute significantly to the economic and social development of Ningde. The important work that we are engaged in today, which is to alleviate poverty and generate wealth, would not succeed without the active participation of the She people or the joint efforts of all ethnic groups. In short, the great unity of all ethnic groups has been and will always be an indispensable guarantee that our efforts to build socialism are successful.

It is our duty to effectively handle issues that involve ethnic minorities. The Party and the state have consistently supported ethnic minorities and minority areas in their efforts to develop economic and cultural undertakings. This is neither charity nor one-way assistance. It benefits all parties. The Han ethnic group helps minority groups, and ethnic minorities help the Han people as well. The state supports the development of minority areas, and minority areas contribute to the construction of the country.

During their long history, the She people have developed a rich, local culture that has been recognized across the nation. It is a bright pearl in the cultural treasure box of Ningde. We take pride in all the distinctions and advantages that make up the culture of the She people. By effectively handling ethnic affairs, we can preserve these distinctive features and play up these advantages.

2. Develop a strategic policy to alleviate poverty in minority areas

The 13th CPC National Congress identified "one central task, two basic points"[5] as our guiding thought to implement this phase of our strategy to alleviate poverty and generate wealth in minority areas. Currently, our work with ethnic minorities is how to meet their demand of accelerating economic growth and cultural progress of minority areas. The acceleration and development of their region's economy will help ethnic minorities to narrow the gap in development between them and the Han people, or better catch up with the Han people. Only then will inequalities be truly eradicated, and all ethnic groups enjoy shared prosperity. This is our touchstone when we handle ethnic affairs in a socialist country like ours. This has been the focus of our work with ethnic minorities, and it remains the core of their fundamental interests.

The equality of all ethnic groups is the cornerstone of Marxist ethnic theories, and the center of our ethnic policies. The economic basis of socialism, combined with the socialist political system that eliminates the oppression of ethnic minorities, fundamentally guarantees the equality of all ethnic groups. Nevertheless, we should also recognize that real equality can only be achieved when everyone enjoys the same level of economic and cultural development. National efforts to eradicate poverty have begun to shift toward minority areas. In the 1990s, poverty alleviation work in areas inhabited by the She people in Ningde will go from ensuring that people have adequate food and clothing to achieving moderate prosperity by focusing on economic development and opening up. We need to consolidate and build on the achievements we made in the 1980s, and do our best to quickly narrow the economic gaps that exist between She areas and other more developed regions in Ningde, the province, and the country. We should start by playing up their strengths and removing obstacles to development, so that She areas can continue to optimize factors of production. We want to establish an economic mechanism that best suits the level of productivity in minority areas, so that they develop at a rate that is higher than the provincial average.

Our policy on poverty alleviation must be based on the real situation in minority areas. What is the real situation? First, poverty is still widespread in She areas of Ningde. Statistics in 1985 show that there were 16,000 impoverished She households, accounting for 50% of all farming households. After three years' work to reduce poverty, 75% of the impoverished households have been lifted out of poverty. Nevertheless, this percentage is still lower than the prefectural average of 87.3%. More than 4,000 minority households in Ningde are still trying to escape poverty. Furthermore, many of those who now live above the poverty line are still at risk of falling below it again for various reasons, including natural disasters, errors in production or business operation, and lack of sustained improvement. It is important to remember that the overall portion of people who have been lifted out of poverty is still too low. Moreover, escaping poverty is not the same thing as enjoying prosperity. Second, the majority of She villages have yet to develop a commodity economy, and some villages still live in a natural or semi-natural economy. Third, the She people tend to live in remote corners of Ningde, where there is poor transportation, limited access to information, and a shortage of technology and talent. For this reason, these areas are underdeveloped and underutilized, despite their rich natural endowments of vast mountains and fertile soil. The situations in these three aspects should be the main points we must consider when we formulate strategies and policies for poverty alleviation and wealth creation in minority areas.

At present, we should pay special attention to the following issues.

First, while state support and assistance are integral to the economic development of minority areas, the financial resources of the state are limited, and Ningde remains a poor region. Therefore, it is not realistic to hope for more outside investment to support the economic development of minority areas. Instead, state support and assistance are meant to empower minority areas to drive their own development. Their own efforts must play the decisive role in the development of their own communities. They must align their own level of productivity with outside support in order to get the most benefits. In other words, they need to improve their own productivity and enhance their ability to attract and absorb support from outside for their communities. In practice, this is reflected in the complementary capabilities that a minority area nurtures before accepting state assistance. We cannot simply hold out our hands and expect the state to fill them with cash. If subsidies are viewed as isolated injections of funds, without any corresponding investment to expand their impact, then the projects they support will collapse once those subsidies stop.

She areas of Ningde should start with their long-term interests, and then gain outside assistance to work in tandem with their own efforts. In other words, they should increase their own productivity and then integrate it with outside support. More assistance may be needed during the initial stages; however, just like weaning a lamb, this financial assistance is only temporary. A lamb must develop the skills needed to live independently after it is weaned. Moreover, She communities should have some complementary production capabilities in place before accepting state assistance. For example, the state invests in minority areas to help them build hydropower stations that will provide communities with electricity for residential and business use. However, if the said minority area cannot provide the funding for the construction of lines of power linking every household, then that area will not benefit from the state's investment. Finally, She areas need to be able to absorb technology. Otherwise, many investments will fail to bring into play their benefits.

While accepting aid and support from the state, She communities need to become more adept at driving their own development. In other words, local conditions should guide their attempts to develop productivity. They should tap natural resources as they open up new markets. They should embark on a development path that integrates markets, technology, and resources suitable for mountainous She areas.

Second, we need to give ethnic minorities the support they need to free themselves from the closed and unitary natural economy, and make the transformation to a commodity economy. This will create virtuous cycles in their regional economies. From now on, funds to alleviate poverty should be directed primarily at supporting minority areas, helping them set up business entities at the village and township levels, and empowering them to drive their own economic development. We should encourage the use of science and technology to alleviate poverty, promote applied technical training, and train some leading technicians and skilled workers. This will help people in She areas master practical skills. We also encourage relevant departments to form partnerships with impoverished She areas in poverty alleviation. When I first arrived in Ningde, I went to Tanyang Village, which has been working in partnership with the Ethnic Affairs Commission of Fu'an County. People in the village have managed to lift themselves out of poverty by planting Kyoho grapes. In 1988, their per capita income reached 700 yuan. This is a great success story.

Third, we should take full advantage of the natural conditions in minority areas while leveraging resources from outside. Ethnic minorities should establish their own economic models for planting, raising livestock, and processing agricultural products based on their own unique conditions. For example, the areas can develop backyard economies in which individual households plant orchards, grow tea plantations, open their farms to tourism, and build ponds, all on a small scale. They can also put significant efforts into building rural enterprises. We should encourage the integration of short-, medium-, and long-term projects, and the coordination of farming, raising livestock, and processing agricultural products. I visited several villages, including Badi and Chongru, which developed their economies by raising pigs and cultivating mushrooms and tea. These are medium- and short-term projects that require little investment but promise quick returns. Of course, areas should also invest in medium- and long-term projects to sustain future development.

Certain traditions and factors have constrained economic growth in minority areas, causing them to remain underdeveloped. While there is little investment in science and technology, poor transportation, and a shortage of skilled personnel, these areas are rich in natural resources. On the contrary, economies in areas populated mainly by the Han people have tended to be more developed. These areas enjoy greater capacity in science and technology, easy access to transportation, and an abundance of skilled workers, but they lack natural resources. This contrast determines that She areas in Ningde should adopt "two-way opening up" and "two-way development."

"Two-way opening up" means opening up to both domestic and international markets. On the one hand, minority areas should actively compete in their own regional markets and in the markets of economically developed coastal areas. They should encourage more investment from outside and establish stronger lateral ties at home. Bringing in information, capital, technology, and talent from outside benefits both the investor and the recipient as their advantages complement each other. On the other hand, minority areas should also participate in competition and exchange on the international market, develop an export-oriented economy, and promote the comprehensive development of their regional economy.

"Two-way development" refers to the coordinated development of markets and natural resources. Minority areas should develop natural resources found in the "mountains, seas, and fields" of the region, create processing and tertiary industries that take advantage of these natural resources, and promote the growth of the commodity economy in rural areas. Minority areas should also develop markets and expand commodity circulation channels. They should encourage the development of farming, animal husbandry and corresponding processing industries that will meet the needs of the market. These steps will provide more opportunities for the large surplus labor force that exists in the vast countryside, especially in She communities, to use their skills.

When basing our development on local resources, we must establish a strategic thinking that is "market-oriented," and formulate a development strategy that is focused on "markets, technology, and natural resources." We all recognize that natural resources are not the same as economic resources, and natural advantages do not equate to economic advantages. Only after being integrated with the market do natural resources become economic resources. Their effective use and development must focus on the needs of society and the goods thus produced must meet the needs of the market. Therefore, when using natural resources to develop commodity production, minority areas must first consider the needs of the market and the region's technical capacity before attempting to draw on their natural advantages. We should also keep in mind that natural resources might not generate immediate economic benefits. Oftentimes, they require several rounds of development and added value before finally demonstrating any comprehensive economic benefits. For example, many local products are created using raw materials that come from wild plants. If these plants are simply harvested (picked) in their natural state, they may not bring in a favorable exchange value. Products that are geared toward the market and processed with appropriate technology will boost use and exchange values that are significantly higher than the value of their raw materials. These kinds of products will bring in markedly higher profits. Clearly, focusing on "markets, technology, and resources" enables minority areas to develop natural resources in ways that are more sophisticated. It increases their efficiency in utilizing natural resources and improves their overall profitability.

The She areas in Ningde developed later than others in the region. Not only did they have a shaky foundation, they had to contend with a large number of restrained conditions. Nevertheless, these areas have great potential for developing a commodity economy. Before they can successfully alleviate poverty and become prosperous, She areas must consider ways to become more economically independent and increase the vitality of their economic development. Then, they can embark on a path that best suits their needs. This requires instituting conceptual change and improving the quality of workers. It requires taking advantage of natural resources in the "mountains, seas and fields," and focusing on the development of township and village enterprises. These concerted efforts will promote the full-scale development of the rural economy and bring about a fundamental shift from poverty to prosperity.

3. Craft a strategy to train ethnic minorities to become officials

Mao Zedong pointed out that it is impossible to thoroughly address issues involving ethnic minorities and to completely isolate reactionaries without a large number of ethnic minority Communist officials. Government officials with a minority background have a natural connection to their own ethnic groups. They are good at communicating the wishes and requests of ethnic minorities. They act as bridges when policies are implemented in minority areas. Such officials play a special and irreplaceable role in carrying out specific work in minority communities. The recruiting and training of officials from among ethnic minorities is not only an important policy of the Party, it is the key to managing issues involving ethnic minorities. Here in Ningde, we still have too few ethnic minorities serving as government officials. This problem demands our attention and action.

We need to concentrate on three areas. First, we should continue to nurture officials with minority background and improve their competence. Second, we should develop a reserve force of government officials for future from ethnic minorities. Third, we should ensure that officials from ethnic minorities constitute a certain proportion of the leadership at the prefecture and county levels. Villages and towns with more than 1,000 ethnic minority residents should have at least one person with a minority background in a deputy leadership position. The training of ethnic minority people to become leading officials must become part of our long-term strategy. We should train young students who show signs of talent while still in primary or middle school. We should improve primary and middle schools exclusively for ethnic minorities, enhance the quality of their education, and expand their scope of knowledge. Areas without ethnic minority schools should make a point of enrolling more ethnic minority students to help prepare them for college. In addition, measures should be adopted to help colleges and vocational schools train students for specific minority areas or enroll students who will work in designated minority areas after graduation.

4. Preserve and develop ethnic cultures

Every ethnic minority has unique cultural traditions that distinguish it from others. These cultural traditions form an ethical and moral wealth that has been built up generation after generation, serving as both a source and a driving force for development. When putting together, the distinctive cultural traditions of ethnic minorities enrich civilization of the humankind. China is a big family made up of multiple ethnicities. The culture of the Chinese people is an amalgam of every ethnic culture in China.

Over their long history, the She people have created a rich culture that they treasure. Indeed, their culture is a valuable jewel in the collective wealth of our nation. The She culture has played a positive role in the preservation and development of the She people. During the course of socialist modernization, we must also ensure that the She culture is carried forward. First, we should preserve their outstanding traditions. The She language, songs, costumes, and personal adornments constitute the most basic aspects of their culture and should be preserved. When I visited several She villages, I learned that some young girls didn't know how to style their hair in the traditional way. Some could not even speak the She language. It is especially important that young people are able to carry forward the cultural traditions of their group. Second, we must lose no time in studying, exploring, and documenting the cultural heritage of the She people. We should coordinate resources to conduct in-depth studies of their songs, folklore, proverbs, music, dance, and stories. Then, absorb the best parts and try to apply them to the present day. For example, I think the She people have a unique way of singing and dancing. They have such grace. When they sing at traditional gatherings, their songs can be refined to an even higher artistic level. We should build a museum devoted to the She people, set up a research institute to study their culture, and organize song and dance troupes to share their traditions. Taking these steps will enrich our nation's multiethnic culture. Third, we should try to broaden the cultural life of the She people and encourage them to participate in healthy recreational and sporting activities. We should establish and improve ethnic culture offices, cultural centers, village clubs, cultural activity rooms, and reading rooms. In short, we should explore various methods and channels at multiple levels to develop modern cultural enterprises for ethnic minorities.

5. Strengthen leadership in ethnic affairs

Ethnic affairs are complicated. This type of work covers a wide range of issues in which policies play an important role. Leaders at every level of the Party and the government should take an interest in issues that concern ethnic minorities. They should respect the lawful rights and interests of ethnic minorities, and show concern for them in terms of economy, culture, education, and public health. They should take concrete steps to help ethnic minorities solve urgent problems.

Officials working at every level of ethnic affairs commissions and civil affairs departments should embody a strong spirit of service. They are the bridges that link the Party and the government with ethnic minorities. They are the advisors and assistants to Party committees and the government on issues involving ethnic minorities. As such, they should make it their solemn duty to improve work on minority issues. They should go deep into areas where She people live to understand their everyday life, report and resolve their problems, and integrate the reality with the Party's principles and policies on ethnic issues.

Notes

[1] Source of English translation (slightly revised here): Mao Zedong, *On the Correct Handling of Contradictions Among the People* (Beijing: Foreign Language Press, 1966), 1. – *Tr.*

[2] Ye Fei (1914-1999) was a military strategist and statesman. Born in Quezon Province, the Philippines, his family was from Nan'an, Fujian Province. He was the only person to have ever held dual nationality and served as a general in the fight to establish the People's Republic of China.

[3] A native of Yizhang, Hunan Province, Zeng Zhi (1911-1998) was an outstanding member of the Communist Party of China. She was a proletarian revolutionary who proved her loyalty countless times as she fought for the Communist cause.

[4] A native of Shouning, Fujian Province, Fan Shiren (1909-1986) was an outstanding member of the Communist Party of China who proved his loyalty countless times fighting for the Communist cause.

[5] "One central task, two basic points" are the basis of the Party line to guide policymaking during the primary stage of socialism. "One central task" refers to economic development; "two basic points" refer to the Four Cardinal Principles and the reform and opening-up policy.

Real Options for Drafting and Implementing an Industrial Policy

July 1989

The regional economy of Ningde Prefecture has been underdeveloped for a variety of reasons, of which the lack of a coherent industrial structure in impoverished areas is an important one. The existing industrial structure has made it difficult for businesses to strengthen their links in production and coordination, to form cooperation within the region, and to make quality local products on a large scale. As a result, we have failed to take full advantage of the coastal areas and have been slow to tap natural resources in the mountains. Therefore, it is vital that we develop and implement a policy that will improve the industrial structure.

Now is a golden opportunity to adjust the industrial structure. There are two general requirements for managing economic conditions and rectifying the economic order. First, we must regulate overall volume. We can accomplish this by controlling excessively rapid expansion of the economy and cooling overheated demand. Second, we need to engage in restructuring. We can do this by strengthening the development of the agricultural sector, basic industries, infrastructure, and the technology industry, while at the same time relying less on processing industries. This is consistent with our urgent need to draft an industrial policy. One can look at an industrial policy as the macro regulation aimed at having a rational allocation of resources among industries, optimizing the industrial structure and improving

134

the quality of industries. What kind of industrial policy should we implement in Ningde? The answer has to be found after considering the actual situations in Ningde.

First, the industrial policy should be based on the regional conditions for "big agriculture." Not only is agriculture the largest sector in Ningde, most of its industrial output value also comes from industries that process agricultural and side-line products. Industrial development in Ningde has been and will continue to be dependent on agriculture for a very long time. Therefore, a sound industrial policy should focus on leveraging agriculture to develop industry, while also using the developing industrial sector to support agriculture.

Second, the industrial policy should be based on the actual strengths and realities of our region. A rational industrial structure corresponds to specific times, places, and conditions. In order to optimize the industrial structure, the industrial policy must be formulated on the basis of the given conditions of the region in question. The current level of economic development in Ningde can be summarized as follows. Per capita income remains at the subsistence level. More than 70% of the region's large labor force works in agriculture. Out of more than 1,000 industrial enterprises at the township-level or higher, only ten reported output values that exceeded RMB10 million. Financial and material resources are limited, and capital is in short supply. Economic conditions such as these signal that the industrial structure needs to be more balanced. The primary objective should be to rationalize the industrial structure, not blindly pursue "high standards." When adjusting the industrial structure, we should not be concerned about temporary gains or losses for a specific project in a specific location. Instead, we should focus on long-term effects and development goals. When drafting an industrial policy, it is important to concentrate on improving economic efficiency. This helps unearth existing potential and possible advantages, and emphasizes the development of the agricultural sector, basic industries, and infrastructure. We should adopt preferential policies for key construction or technological transformation projects that have already been identified, ensure they are adequately funded, and strive for early completion, early production, and early results.

Third, the industrial policy should cater to local conditions and make the most of regional advantages. The natural resources found in the mountains and waters of Ningde vary widely, yet the industrial structure of the region presents a largely even distribution. In other words, different areas of the region have similar industrial structures despite their very different resources. This has made cooperation among businesses in the region difficult and has allowed opportunities to play up natural advantages go to waste. When drafting an industrial policy for the region, we should focus on the advantages that different areas have to offer. After all, "clouds follow the dragon, and winds follow the tiger."[1] We need to determine the priority for industrial structure adjustment in different areas, look for good starting points, and then ensure that the industrial structures of different areas parallel the distribution of resources.

Fourth, the industrial policy should be based on self-reliance, and the development of industry should conform to its self-balancing capacity. In light of the realities of the nation and the province, it is unrealistic for us to look outside Ningde for the strength and financial resources to adjust our industrial structure and develop our industry. We need to be the ones to put our house in order. We need to adapt our industrial development to our capacity for self-balancing. Self-balancing is a broad concept that includes the balanced integration of capital, technology, talent, and resources. In the process of self-balancing, we should deal with urgent matters and low-hanging fruits first, apply experience gained from individual projects to a broader context, and make steady incremental progress. We should prioritize future industries and products, and then sort industries and products into groups: those that should be supported and encouraged, and those that should be restricted or prohibited. We should extend different treatment to different industries. While preferential treatment should be given to bottleneck industries that restrict our region's industrial development, limitations should be strictly applied to the glut of general processing industries. In addition to keeping their numbers in check, processing industries should go through internal restructuring in order to moderate their scale and rationalize their structure.

Here is the principle we should follow. We should consider from the perspective of demand and the consumption of resources. Processing industries that make slow-selling products and consume a great deal of resources must be reduced or outright prohibited. Industries that make quick-selling products and consume low levels of resources should be given strong support. For industries that either make quick-selling products and consume large amounts of resources, or make slow-selling products and consume fewer resources, we should help them reduce consumption or adjust product structures.

We should also consider from another perspective: the degree of processing and the consumption of resources. Industries that are not process-intensive but consume lots of resources must be shut down. Industries that are process-intensive but consume small amounts of resources must be given strong support. Industries that are either process-intensive and consume a lot of resources, or not process-intensive and consume few resources, should be given the support they need either to reduce consumption levels or increase the depth and precision of processing.

Key resources freed up from the contraction of the processing industry should be directed toward the agricultural sector, basic industries, and infrastructure. In the near future, such resources should be invested in infrastructure for energy, transportation, and communications, and in raw material industry. This will gradually mitigate problems brought about by lagging basic industries.

Energy construction should focus on building the three lines for power transmission and transformation, and integrating the development and utilization of hydropower resources. I have always maintained, "as soon as you have money, invest it in developing power station." We can raise funds to build small power stations, and then attract foreign capital to build medium power stations. Eventually, hydropower will become the dominant source of electricity in Ningde, and the electric power industry can be integrated with the provincial power grid to accommodate peak usage.

Transportation should be focused on resurfacing existing roads, extending roads to connect counties, and constructing new roads in the countryside. We should designate Saiqi a shipping hub, and speed up initial plans to expand the 3,000-ton wharf in Xiabaishi. We should start an ocean shipping fleet, open up long-distance and peripheral shipping lines, and create a shipping network. We should accelerate the development of postal and telecommunications industries with the goal of increasing the level of automation in the regional network, in order to speed up the development of key areas, improve the level of communication in intermediate zones, and develop services in impoverished rural areas.

Fifth, the industrial policy should rationally select leading industries based on their regional advantages. Not only do the natural resources found in coastal and mountainous counties differ, they also have different labor forces, transportation networks, energy sources, raw materials, technological conditions, and economic bases. Therefore, when choosing a leading (pillar) industry, we should try to make the most of their advantages and play down their weaknesses. It makes sense for counties and cities on the coast to utilize two kinds of resources and two kinds of markets, while counties located in the mountains follow the resource transformation model. The current state of our industrial structure and its development conditions indicate that we should take steps to establish three leading industries. More specifically, we should prioritize the consolidation and development of a foodstuff industry, give preferred development to a textile and light industry, and encourage the rapid formation of an electro-mechanical industry of considerable scale. Every county has some competitive products that have good prospects for development. For example, Gutian has the deep processing of mushrooms, and Xiapu has massage tools and three-vegetable[2] processing. Fu'an has electrical machinery and ferroalloys, and Zherong has pharmaceuticals. For key products like these that have sufficient supplies of raw materials and ready markets, we should form business consortiums and enterprise groups to promote specialization and coordination. This helps build economies of scale through mass production, which in turn increases profitability.

The five points that I have just discussed may be considered a basic platform for establishing our industrial policy. If we stick to it, I am convinced that the industrial policy of Ningde will not be like "water without a source" or "a tree without roots." After thorough research, communication, and coordination, we can forecast economic trends of our region within the macroeconomic environment. We can then establish a unified plan to guide and implement our industrial policy for the short-, medium-, and long-term.

Short-term objectives: Small- and medium-sized processing enterprises that contribute little to government revenue, employ not many people, and have no better market for their products must limit or cease production. They can be absorbed through mergers, leasing, auctions, reorganization, etc. In light of a long-term strategy, we should identify pillar industries and key products in Ningde, concentrate limited economic resources, and invest in these priority sectors, so as to provide support to them in times of difficulty when the markets are sluggish and lay the foundation for future development.

Medium-term objectives: Examine pillar industries and key products for links to other industries, and encourage product restructuring in related industries. Form a "radial" system centered around pillar industries that drive the development of related industries, and then upgrade technology and equipment at key enterprises in pillar industries and key sectors of related industries. While further reducing the production of slow-selling, disadvantaged goods by general processing industries, we should develop local specialty products, peripheral products, and products for basic industries, increase the degree of specialization in production, and enhance vitality and competitiveness. We should also encourage the tertiary industry that provides services to manufacturing, and improve the soft environment.

Long-term objectives: Build on the foundation created by short- and medium-term objectives to further leverage the existing capacity of economic resources and encourage growth in selected sectors. We should expand the adoption of advanced technology and equipment in pillar and related industries, improve the system of industrial organization, and further develop the tertiary industry. Ultimately, we will reach our goals of optimizing our industrial structure and improving industrial quality.

Notes

[1] Source of English translation: *The I Ching: The Book of Changes*, trans. James Legge, (New York: Dover Publications, Inc., 1963), 411. – *Tr.*

[2] The three vegetables – seaweed, nori, and mustard root – are common agricultural by-products in Xiapu County.

Breaking Through Difficulties
– Thoughts on Developing Township Enterprises in Poor Areas

October 1989

With the rapid rise of township enterprises as reform and opening up surge ahead, such enterprises have become a new force in the development of rural commodity economy. They play an increasingly important role in political, economic, and social life in impoverished areas. The opening-up and development practice in Ningde in recent years is eloquent proof of this.

We should clearly understand, though, that with the gradual deepening of rectification, township enterprises are facing a critical period of survival and development. Why do I say "critical"? First, after several years of rapid development, township enterprises are now entering a stage of consolidation, improvement, and optimization. Over the next two years, the number of such enterprises won't increase much as we must focus on improving their quality. Second, in the current weak market and monetary tightening, coupled with a shortage of raw materials and energy, township enterprises are being forced to find new ways to prosper through adjusting their product structure. Third, the weaknesses of township enterprises were exposed during their first phase of development; they need to improve themselves and enhance their competitiveness to facilitate their own future development.

We say that township enterprises have reached a critical stage of success or failure because we want people to view their development from a macro perspective.

Under the two-tiered system of unified management combined with independent household operations, township enterprises today are jointly operated by a township, a town, a village, or a group of farming households. In other words, township enterprises are collectively-owned, established by farmers, and have the characteristics of rural social organizations. They are socialist in nature and are positive and progressive entities. Some people see township enterprises as a product of market regulation only. This is a misunderstanding. Township enterprises embody the principles of socialism. They not only essentially promote public ownership of means of production, they also fundamentally implement the principle of "to each according to his work." Due to the socialist nature of township enterprises, they must be directly or indirectly subject to the socialist macroeconomic operating mechanism of planned, proportional development. Of course, township enterprises are "people-owned" enterprises run collectively by farmers and are different than "state-owned" enterprises. Their production, supply, and sales are not directly included in state planning. They participate in the market. Thus, the most notable feature of township enterprise operations is that it is subject to both macro planning and market regulation.

If we grasp this point, the direction for the development of township enterprises becomes clear: interaction and coordination between the law of planned, proportional development and the law of value, and common guidance by the two laws. Specifically, township enterprise development strategy, overall resource allocation, overall social supply and demand, and interest rates, tax rates, and exchange rates are subject to the regulation of the planned economy. The production and operation of the enterprises can follow economic interests and the law of value, and they can freely and directly participate in market exchange and competition.

Of course, the planned regulation of township enterprises is different from the planned administration of state-owned enterprises. First, the state does not directly intervene in the economic operations of township enterprises, and cannot issue mandatory plans. Second, the state focuses mainly on the overall planning for township enterprises, and regulates the scale and speed of their development on a macro basis. Third, in the administration of township enterprises, the state uses mainly economic methods to carry out indirect planned regulation. Fourth, township enterprises have some flexibility within the planned regulation, demonstrated by the fact that they have room for change within the overall operational direction of the plan and the ability to make timely corrections to their own plan.

In short, the development of township enterprises must be in line with the macroeconomic development plans and be consistent with the overall pace of economic development. In this context, township enterprises in poor areas must also fully understand their own weaknesses, and work hard to adapt and improve these as they grow.

Based on the above analysis, township enterprises must know where to ground themselves in the development process.

First, they must be grounded in their locality. Only a native enterprise will have the strong local flavor of Ningde. The township enterprises of Ningde began with farming, animal husbandry and processing. Actual practice over the last few years has proven that this initial direction is on target and the development process is healthy. Our township enterprises have good mountain- and sea-based resources to draw from, and those who take advantage of these resources will find a broader path to growth. We have already seen benefit in this regard. Some township enterprises engage in the processing and development of mountain- and sea-based resources, including tea, fruit, bamboo, and marine products. They produce a number of products with local characteristics such as Xiapu County's spicy mustard tuber, Fuding County's betel nut taro powder, Shouning County's malted coixseed, and Fu'an City's mushroom floss and orange drinks. These products are sold inside and outside the province and loved by consumers. Some counties are quickly developing and using mineral resources like kaolin, pyrophyllite, perlite, tungsten ore, and diabase as very marketable products.

Second, township enterprises must be grounded in agriculture to provide services to "big agriculture." With the development of what we call "big agriculture," township enterprises can engage in the related services of processing, storage, packaging, transportation, supply, and marketing for the agriculture, forestry, animal husbandry, sideline production, and fishery industries. These enterprises will be vibrant and have broad prospects for growth.

Third, township enterprises must be grounded in specialty products to survive and develop in niche markets. In this regard, Ningde has opened up a path by developing a number of chemical, electromechanical, and electronic enterprises. Examples include Xiapu County's Songhe-brand MSG, Fuding County's electronic components, and Zhouning County's activated carbon products. But we must be very cautious as we create "technology- and capital-intensive" township enterprises, because we do not have advantages in this area. We should play to our strengths and allow for the survival of the fittest.

Fourth, township enterprises must be grounded in looking "overseas." Ningde is located on the coast of Fujian Province, and Ningde and Xiapu counties are listed among China's coastal economic open zones. As we further our opening up to the outside world, in recent years Ningde is exporting more and more woven bamboo products, candied fruit, and mushrooms to overseas markets. This should point to the direction for the development of township enterprises across the whole prefecture.

In conclusion, as long as we ground ourselves in the realities of Ningde and strengthen our guidance, coordination, and support for township enterprises in our impoverished areas, I am sure they will be able to find a way out of their current predicament and embrace brighter prospects, as described in a well-known poem:

When one doubts whether there is a way out from the endless mountains and rivers,

One suddenly finds a village shaded in soft willows and bright flowers.[1]

Notes

[1] See Lu You, "A Trip to Mountain West Village." A native of Shanyin, Yue Prefecture (modern Shaoxing, Zhejiang Province), Lu You (1125-1210) was a poet of the Southern Song Dynasty (1127-1279) who was celebrated for his patriotism.

Let the People's Congress Play a Bigger Role in Ningde's Development

November 1989

Ningde's development is inseparable from the work of the people's congress. In recent years, the people's congresses at all levels in Ningde have made significant accomplishments and played an increasingly important role in the political life of the whole region. In our new situation, we should continue to follow the guiding principles of the central authorities and further explore the rules of the people's congress work, sum up our experience, consolidate our achievements, and strive to take the work of the people's congress to a new level.

We must first continue to raise awareness of the work of people's congress. Our system of people's congress, which was gradually established and developed during the war years, is China's fundamental political system. What we need now is to further strengthen and improve this system, rather than to doubt or weaken it. As Deng Xiaoping clearly pointed out, "In the reform of the political structure, one thing is certain: we must adhere to the system of the people's congresses instead of practicing the separation of the judicial, executive and legislative powers on the American pattern."[1] Previously, there was a tendency toward wholesale Westernization and the dilution of the role of the people's congress. This should be severely criticized. To adhere to the people's congress system is to uphold the Four Cardinal Principles[2] in our political system. Our officials at all levels and Party members must have a correct understanding of our state

146

institutions, state system, and political system. That includes building socialist democratic politics, keeping close ties between the Party and the people, strengthening and improving the Party's leadership of the organs of state power, and safeguarding, respecting, and supporting the work of the people's congress, allowing it to play an important role. We must strengthen public awareness of the nature, status, mandate, and role of the people's congress. Some people's use of doggerel phrases like "big sign, empty structure, old men" and "three levels of organs acting like a rubber stamp" only demonstrates their one-sided and ambiguous understanding of the people's congress. It remains our long-term task to publicize the accomplishments of the people's congress, summarize its experiences, and improve the public's awareness about it.

Second, we must do a good job in handling the relationships between Party committee, people's congress, and government. The relationships between these three institutions are clear. Party committee should place the work of the people's congress on important agendas, take on its own leadership responsibility effectively, and constantly improve its leadership of the people's congress. Within the framework of the Constitution and laws, it should be adept at carrying out the Party' intentions through the effective work of the Party leading group of the people's congress and the exemplary role of the Party members who serve as deputies to the people's congress, to realize the Party's political ideas by relying on and mobilizing the people. Party committees at all levels should actively support the people's congress in exercising its powers according to law, and should build the prestige of the people's congress and help to solve real problems. Major decisions to be made by the people's congress should be submitted to it in a timely manner, using statutory procedures to turn the decisions into the state's will. Once resolutions or statutes are formulated, government departments must conscientiously implement them, and Party organizations and Party members must take the lead in the implementation. We must optimize the selection of standing committee members of local people's congress and look for both ability and integrity in selecting people's congress officials. We must pay attention to the age and knowledge structure of members who form a leadership group. At the same time, we must do what we can to create the necessary conditions for the work of the people's congress, focusing in particular on the treatment of people's congress officials in politics, work, and life. The appointment and removal of officials is an important issue in the relationship between Party committee and people's congress. As long as the two entities share common principles, consult with each other, and keep each other informed, they are capable of reaching consensus. In short, personnel appointments and removals should reflect both the principle of the Party in administering officials and the supervisory role of the people's congress and its deputies.

The relationships between the people's congress and government, the people's court, and the people's procuratorate are also very clear. Supervision is the sacred duty entrusted by the Constitution to the people's congress, which must confidently exercise its supervisory powers to ensure that the Constitution, laws, and regulations in its respective jurisdictions are observed and implemented. Government, the people's court, and the people's procuratorate should consciously accept supervision by the people's congress, seriously implement the congress' resolutions and decisions. They should also value and act upon proposals, comments, and suggestions put forward by deputies to the people's congress.

The supervision of the people's congress is to better support and promote the work of the government, and it should be positive supervision. The people's congress should address major and crucial matters, rather than taking on any matter regardless of its importance or exceeding the scope of its work. In making decisions on major issues like annual plans or fiscal policy, the people's congress can get involved early to study the matters, consult and communicate with the relevant parties frequently in order to narrow differences to achieve consensus. In short, when Party committee, the people's congress, and government adhere to common goals and interests and act in accordance with the Party Constitution and the national Constitution, we can expect good relationship among the three. Even if problems arise occasionally, it will be easy to address them properly.

Third, we must address major and critical issues and actively develop the functional role of the people's congress. The new situation means higher demands of the people's congress. It requires us to stand higher, broaden our perspective, master more circumstances, and make more accurate analyses. The people's congress has a lot of work to do. As we face a multitude of tasks, we must remain grounded in reality, make careful arrangements, focus on the key issues of the national economy and social development, focus on the issues that are most concerned to the people, conscientiously exercise powers according to the rules and features of the work, and achieve tangible results. Currently, the focus should be on rectification and deepening reform, and the major, difficult, and hot issues. In 1990, the task of rectification and deepening reform will be extremely arduous. Unstable elements are still quite prominent in our prefecture, and we also face many hot issues such as relocation of residents as a result of reservoir building, unauthorized loan agencies, underground religious activities, production and work stoppage in factories, and decline in the prices of shrimps, mushrooms, tea, and other mainstay products. Failure to resolve these issues properly will affect stability and unity, and interfere with rectification and deepening reform. Local people's congresses should increase their investigation and research of such matters. After having a clear understanding of the issues and getting a handle on the situation, they should focus on a few high-profile problems that have impact on the overall work, come up with decisions about them in accordance with legal procedures, and carefully monitor the government's implementation. In this way, we can effectively promote the prefecture's move from poverty to prosperity, revive the economy so that it will continue to make coordinated and healthy progress forward. The investigative work of the people's congress has its notable features: one, it focuses on major economic and social development issues; two, it involves a large number of matters that are of great concern to the people; three, there are many issues with respect to the perfection of laws and regulations; and four, it requires a large amount of investigation and research on democratic politics such as elections and grassroots governance. The study and resolution of these problems will help to promote all of our work, and there is reason to hope that the people's congress will conduct better and more solid research.

Fourth, we must build up the capacity of the people's congress to improve itself. In recent years, the people's congresses at all levels have constantly learned from their experiences and overcome difficulties in exploring the way forward. But it still takes a great effort for the people's congress to adapt to a developing situation and improve itself. Improving itself means building up its philosophy, systems, organization, institutions, work committees, among other things. By improving itself and constantly improving its ability to discuss and examine matters, the people's congress will further its role as local power organs.

There is another meaningful task in strengthening the self-improvement of the people's congress, that is, to improve the educational level and proficiency of the people's deputies, who are the bond and bridge linking the Party and the state with the people. Let the deputies play their role to the full is key to the better work of the people's congress. Our prefecture has a high proportion of deputies who are farmers with less education, hailing from scattered villages. It is difficult for them to participate in relevant events and activities. We must help them better fulfill their duties, improve their awareness as deputies, and increase their capacity for participation in the deliberation and administration of state affairs. We want the deputies to be active not just during sessions of the people's congress, but also to participate in events and activities before and after sessions. We must have more demand on the work of the people's deputies and maintain close contact with them, organizing inspections and investigations on a regular basis to ensure that they are fully in touch with the people, listening to public opinions, and resolving problems.

Notes

[1] Source of English translation: Deng Xiaoping, "Address to Officers at the Rank of General and Above in Command of the Troops Enforcing Martial Law in Beijing," in *Selected Works of Deng Xiaoping*, vol. 3, trans. the Bureau for the Compilation and Translation of Works of Marx, Engels, Lenin and Stalin Under the Central Committee of the Communist Party of China (Beijing: Foreign Language Press, 1994), 299. – *Tr.*

[2] The Four Cardinal Principles are to adhere to the socialist path, adhere to the people's democratic dictatorship, adhere to the leadership of the Communist Party of China, and adhere to Marxism-Leninism and Mao Zedong Thought. These principles are the foundation of the state, and the political cornerstone for the survival and development of the Party and the nation.

Actively and Steadily Reform the Communist Youth League

October 1989

We have recognized the urgency and necessity of reforming the Communist Youth League. The work of the League is not well suited to addressing the emerging situations and new problems brought about by the reform and opening-up process. The only remedy is to persist in and further the reform. But what kind of reform must we pursue? First of all we must be clear that the nature of the League has not changed. It is still the Party's assistant and reserve pool, which is the most basic prerequisite for its reform. Young people are energetic and ardent about reform. At the mention of "reform," words and phrases such as "colorful, dazzling," and "like a wildfire" would come to their mind. They expect overnight success and want to achieve their objectives in one step. But there are no precedents for our reform, and as economic reform continues, it easily leads to complicated contradictions and problems. The slightest mistake will affect the entire reform effort and even result in losses. So, the reform of the Communist Youth League should be neither "all talk and no action" nor a frenzied storm of activity. Our reform can only be pushed forward actively and steadily. That is, we should have great courage, a steady pace, a resolute attitude, and caution in implementation. Being active and steady are two aspects of the process, and there is a unified dialectical relationship between them. In reforming the League, we must understand and follow a disciplined approach, move ahead step by step, and guard against rashness. The overall design of the reform must include three mutually supporting plans: a plan for the final target, a plan for the transition period, and a plan for step-by-step implementation. We must not expect success in one step.

The principle for reforming the work of the Communist Youth League should be to advance actively and steadily. According to this principle, we need to correctly handle the following issues:

1. Follow the general trend of reform while remaining rooted in local realities. Our nationwide reform and opening up makes new demands on the League, but also brings opportunities and a good environment for its own development. The League must catch the reform train and not be left behind. The reform of the League must keep pace with the times. We must think about the country as a whole while avoiding a one-size-fits-all approach. We must start from the reality on the ground, so that the reform of the League is more suited to local needs. For example, the reform of the League's work in Ningde Prefecture must be based on the realities of this place. Ningde is a poor area, and poverty reduction and making good is the overall strategy for its economy. The reform of the local League organization must address how to serve this strategy. Most young people of Ningde live in rural areas. The League should come up with ideas to help these youths find pathways to prosperity, create opportunities, and provide the conditions for youths to develop their talents. The League organizations must strengthen ties with local township enterprises and government departments. If we can have a few more entrepreneurs emerging from the young people with the help and support of the League, I will consider it a success. To determine whether the reform of a local League organization is going well or not, we must first look to see whether it benefits local poverty alleviation work.

2. Serve the Party's central task while accommodating the characteristics of young people. As the Party's assistant, the Communist Youth League assumes the duties assigned it by the Party and organizes its activities based on the central task of the Party. I believe that this point should be undisputed. China is now in the primary stage

of socialism. The Party's central task is to focus on modernization; its basic points are to uphold the Four Cardinal Principles and reform and opening up. The League must therefore base its thinking, work arrangements, and planning on the Party's basic line; otherwise it will go off course. At the same time, we should also consider the age characteristics of the League members. The physiology, psychology, interests, demands, and other characteristics of youth are unlike those of either children or middle-aged people. In his article, "The Youth League in Its Work Must Take the Characteristics of Youth into Consideration," Mao Zedong pointed out, "After all, youth is youth, or else why bother to have a Youth League? Young people are different from adults and so are young women from young men. Disregard these characteristics and you will alienate yourselves from the masses."[1] The League must have its own abundant variety of activities and lively, active way of working, making it thoughtful, informative, and interesting. The League must be youth-oriented, focusing on the majority of young people. Only when the League unites and organizes the entire young generation will they fulfill the Party's mandate to educate youths in Communist ideology and cultivate them to become new Communists with lofty ideals, moral integrity, better education and a good sense of discipline.

3. Safeguard the interests of all the people, but also represent and defend the specific interests of youths. The Communist Youth League must first prioritize the interests of the Party, the nation, and the people. Its work must be conducive to national stability, the unity of people of all ethnic groups, and sustained and stable social and economic development. But this doesn't mean that the League will not speak up for the interests of young people. Only when the League accurately expresses the will of young people can it link closely with them. Only when the League cares for young people in a comprehensive way can it be a more effective bridge between the Party, the government, and the nation's youths. How can the League represent and defend the specific interests of young people? It must eagerly help them to improve their intellectual, moral, scientific, and cultural

qualities, and promote their overall development. It must timely and accurately reflect the voices of young people and protect their legitimate rights and interests. It must do things that benefit young people, making every effort to help them solve their practical problems.

4. Accurately represent the interests of young people, but also educate them and give them correct guidance. While the Communist Youth League represents and defends the interests of young people as described above, it should also address the question of how to guide and educate them. With the reform and opening-up process has come an influx of many foreign things, quite a few of which are corrupt and decadent. Young people are the most vulnerable to the influence of such things. When we talked about preventing the peaceful evolution schemes of imperialist countries, it was by no means "crying wolf"; the "wolf" has indeed come to the door. We cannot give an inch on our socialist position. The League must not give up even an inch of territory. Instead, the League must guide the development of young people. We should ensure that young people study Marxism, Leninism and Mao Zedong Thought, oppose bourgeois liberalization, and decadent feudal ideas. The League can guide youths in studying Marxist philosophy. Young people like to explore. A better command of materialist dialectics will be very helpful to young people in exploring the truth and realizing their talents.

Notes

[1] Source of English translation: Mao Zedong, "The Youth League in Its Work Must Take the Characteristics of Youth into Consideration," in *Selected Works of Mao Tsetung*, vol. 5 (Beijing: Foreign Language Press, 1977), 98. – *Tr.*

Intellectual and Cultural Progress in Impoverished Areas

December 1989

Intellectual and cultural progress is a major aspect of our strategy to eliminate poverty. We have already begun a movement for intellectual and cultural progress in impoverished areas, and should continue to explore the means for advancing such progress in Ningde Prefecture.

I

First of all, it is necessary to clarify our understanding of the following issues.

1. A correct understanding of the relationship between eliminating poverty and intellectual and cultural progress.

The history of social development tells us that there are two types of needs in human life: material needs and cultural needs. Human life understands and transforms the world to meet these two types of needs through material production and cultural production. The pursuit of material and cultural progress is the internal driving force for social progress. Intuitively speaking, to eliminate poverty is the practice of making material progress in poor areas. But true socialism does not only have highly developed productive forces, it must also have a highly developed culture, meaning that while people live a more affluent life, they have developed a high level of moral awareness, as well as good understanding of science and culture. Only then is poverty eliminated in the true sense.

Historical materialism holds that productivity is the ultimate decisive force for all social development, and that relations of production and the superstructure are determined by productivity and must be aligned with the productivity level. But relations of production and the superstructure can also influence productivity. Whether an impoverished area can embark on the road to prosperity ultimately depends on the development of productivity. Concentrating on developing the economy is therefore our most urgent, central task. We believe that the continuing development of the economy will provide a solid material foundation and the conditions for intellectual and cultural progress. We are also aware of the weak base in poor areas, their lack of natural resources, the uneven economic development, and the low level of the commodity economy. For this reason, the process of eliminating poverty will be full of hardships and difficulties. This requires us to focus on economic work while also addressing intellectual and cultural progress, because the latter will help us mobilize the enthusiasm and creativity of officials and people to overcome hardships and difficulties. And, with the public's improved understanding of science and culture and use of science and technology, prosperity will come sooner. Obviously, material and cultural progresses are two sides of the same coin for eliminating poverty in poor areas. They are interrelated, mutually coordinated, and mutually reinforcing. There is a tendency to think in polarized terms that material progress is "hard work" and cultural progress is "soft work." The approach that favors the hard and dismisses the soft, and the idea that the development of commodity production will automatically resolve the problem of poverty, are not in conformity with dialectic methodology. Our guiding thought for eliminating poverty is clear: as we develop commodity production as the fundamental and central task of building a socialist economy, we should also focus on the strategic objective of cleaning up the dregs left over from the old society, purifying the social atmosphere, and improving people's moral awareness and understanding of science and culture.

2. A correct analysis of the history and reality of intellectual and cultural progress: keep up with the good work, correct mistakes, mobilize positive factors and mitigate negative factors.

We have a history of promoting intellectual and cultural progress. In the past years we carried out a civility campaign called "five stresses, four points of beauty, and three things to love,"[1] beginning with cleaning up what was "dirty, disorderly, and bad." We engaged in activities for "a beautiful environment, good order, and quality service" to create culturally advanced towns and villages, as well as a series of educational events about the tradition of the old revolutionary base areas, including the "Love Ningde, Build Ningde" campaign focusing on the "two virtues."[2] In particular, since 1988 we have made remarkable success and achieved visible results. For example, we have "come up with a general plan for cultural progress and focused on the work of grassroots institutions." We have set up a goal and accountability system for intellectual and cultural progress. We have built cultural progress into the "Learn from Lei Feng" campaign for members of the military, police, and the general public. We have also carried out campaigns against pornography[3] and the "six evils."[4] We should clearly understand, though, that the overall social atmosphere has improved, but not substantially. Socialist education is more widespread and in-depth, but some problems left over from the old society are making a comeback. Moral and political awareness in the countryside is still quite weak, and the concept of collectivism is fading. There are a considerable number of people who are illiterate or ignorant of science and the law. Superstition also hinders the spread of science and knowledge. These make it clear that we still face a serious reality not to be taken lightly. Based on a full awareness of our achievements and problems, a dialectical analysis is necessary for our future socialist intellectual and cultural progress, to determine which positive factors can be mobilized, and which negative factors should be mitigated.

A healthy atmosphere of intellectual and cultural progress is permeating the whole country. Due to the serious attention paid by Party organizations at all levels and the extensive participation of the people, the campaign for intellectual and cultural progress has been launched and extended from the initial phase to the full implementation phase. We have accumulated some experience, and a large number of individuals and organizations have emerged as good examples, which have inspired awareness of cultural progress among officials and people. More than a decade of reform and opening up has significantly increased our economic strength and improved the people's standard of living, providing the necessary material condition for intellectual and cultural progress. Moreover, Ningde is an old revolutionary base area with a glorious revolutionary tradition.... Undoubtedly, these are all favorable conditions and positive factors for cultural progress in Ningde.

Of course, we should also note that Ningde has poor geographical conditions and transport facilities. The education level is low in rural areas. A relatively large proportion of people are illiterate or quasi-illiterate, or have never gone beyond elementary school. Superstition, clan forces, and other undesirable feudal practices still have a considerable foundation. Most importantly, a commodity economy has not yet formed, and such an economic base hampers the development of the superstructure. These are the problems we face as we move forward, which are adverse conditions and negative factors hindering cultural progress.

3. Correctly handling the relationship between "breaking down" and "building up" in promoting intellectual and cultural progress.

"Building up" and "breaking down" are two aspects of the same process of intellectual and cultural progress. "Building up" means raising people's moral and political awareness, which requires positive education and promotion. Marxism holds that a scientific socialist awareness cannot spontaneously arise in workers' movements; such awareness can only be instilled from outside. Taking on a Marxist stance, guided by Marxist viewpoints, we will use Marxist methods to reach out to the people, arm the people, and educate the people. An ideology of patriotism, socialism, and collectivism can be rooted in the hearts of the people through continual, painstaking work that raises moral and political awareness. This is "building up." It is fair to say that "building up" is our Party's political advantage. Of course, "building up" alone is not enough; if we do not go after feudalism and capitalist decadence, they will not fall down by themselves. This is where "breaking down" comes in — using criticism to expose the false, the evil, and the ugly, so that they do not win the hearts of the people and will lose their "market." This allows people to consciously resist the invasion of these things in their own thinking. Meanwhile, we must use effective methods like the legal system and administrative measures to persist in the fight against feudalism and capitalist decadence, and to carry out an in-depth and lasting struggle against pornography and vice.

To sum up, "building up" and "breaking down" are both indispensable to intellectual and cultural progress. One cannot build up without breaking down, and vice versa; they complement each other, and are different means of achieving the same end. If we turn a blind eye to and do not fight organized gambling, feudal superstition, and prostitution, how can we talk about "people working on different posts all learn from Lei Feng and foster new practices in all trades"? If we think that we can sit back and relax after taking a few jabs at pornography and vice, such ugly phenomena are likely to resurge at any time in the current situation where moral awareness and the ability to consciously resist temptations have not improved among all.

II

If we want to promote intellectual and cultural progress with the characteristics of Ningde, we must be grounded in the realities of this region while infusing the entire process of eliminating poverty with education on moral awareness and progress in science and culture.

Historical materialism tells us that social consciousness, thoughts and ideas, and scientific and cultural knowledge all arise out of social practices. Eliminating poverty, therefore, is not only a process that transforms our objective world through material progress, but also one that transforms our subjective world through intellectual and cultural progress.

Developing a socialist commodity economy is the fundamental way out of poverty for Ningde. We should integrate developing the economy with enhancing the intellectual and cultural life of the people of Ningde. Socialist commodity economy is characterized by socialist relations of production, dominance of public ownership, and "to each according to his work." This type of economic relations fundamentally rejects the value of "seeking nothing but profit" premised on the bourgeoisie extracting the surplus value created by the workers. Such values are in fact the root of all evils in a capitalist society. Socialist workers are the masters of the means of production; this status determines the equality and mutual assistance between fellow workers. Our new principal value is that, as members of society, individuals must do something for society and make a contribution. Developing the socialist commodity economy is therefore of great practical significance to a new era of cultural and moral progress. Yet this does not mean intellectual and cultural progress comes naturally along with the development of a socialist commodity economy. There is not necessarily a causal relationship between the two; the development of the socialist commodity economy only provides the precondition and possibility for cultural progress.

After all, a commodity economy has some inherent negative attributes. The values of extreme bourgeois selfishness poisons people's minds from time to time. Money worship takes over in some people's thinking. Commodity fetishism has followers in the primary stage of socialism. So, in developing a socialist commodity economy, we must not forget our moral and political work to enhance the cultivation of a socialist spirit and morality. We must consciously encourage people to gradually become aware of the law of commodity production as they participate in the commodity economy, to learn and master knowledge about commodity production and management, and to form ideas, morals, and a lifestyle that conform to modern production and life.

The socialist economy based on public ownership is the leading force in eliminating poverty and achieving prosperity. We should consciously empower this economy to continue to inculcate collectivism and socialism in our citizens. In urban areas, we need to improve the enterprise contract system, and we must enhance the collective economy at the township and village levels. Let the people experience the superiority of the socialist economy based on public ownership, cherish the inseparable relationship between collective and individual interests. This will enhance their sense of responsibility and confidence in building socialism, which will have an immeasurable impact on moral progress and raising political awareness.

Science and technology are key to eliminating poverty. As we promote scientific and technological progress, we should be aware of constantly improving people's understanding of science and culture. Production practice based on scientific and technological progress is the best source of learning for people to improve their knowledge in science and culture. Progress in science and technology can effectively improve workers' competence. In rural areas, we still have a considerable number of illiterate people. To eliminate illiteracy, developing agriculture through science and technology must also be a driving force and motivation. We should emphasize that science can be used not only for production, but also in intellectual and cultural life. We should especially combine scientific and technological progress with socialist education to promote the comprehensive development of rural areas.

Changing old customs and habits and promoting a civilized and healthy lifestyle are necessary conditions for eliminating poverty. We should consciously use policies to regulate people's behavior and guide them onto the track of Communist morality through a healthy lifestyle of civility. Civility and politeness, taking care of public property, observing public order, maintaining social security, showing respect to others, keeping away from anything immoral, respecting the old, and caring for the young are indispensable to a culturally advanced society. Overcoming poverty in the material sense while remaining ignorant in the intellectual and cultural sense is not what we want. What we need is: "When the granaries are full, they will know propriety and moderation. When their clothing and food are adequate, they will know the distinction between honor and shame."[5] After achieving prosperity, some rural areas are now engaging in oversized temple- and mausoleum-building projects to seek blessings from gods and Buddhas. This is worth our careful reflection.

The spirit of old revolutionary base areas is a powerful cultural pillar for eliminating poverty, and we must vigorously carry forward this spirit. People in Ningde's old revolutionary base areas wrote an epic, glorious history during their long revolutionary struggle. Countless martyrs left us with inexhaustible and precious cultural wealth. The revolutionary tradition in those old revolutionary base areas gives Ningde an edge in intellectual and cultural progress. We have unique conditions for integrating Ningde's revolutionary history and tradition in patriotic and Communist education. In poverty elimination and socialist construction, we should inherit the tradition of old revolutionary base areas and carry forward the revolutionary spirit. Everyone should "love the Chinese Communist Party and socialism," and strive to "work hard in the spirit of water droplets drilling through rock, forge ahead, and be selfless in our dedication."

III

Intellectual and cultural progress is the accumulation of the positive results of human transformation of both the subjective world and objective world. It signifies the development level of intellectual and cultural productivity, and is bound to permeate material progress throughout the impoverished areas. It is embodied in every economic, political, cultural, and social aspect of poverty elimination, and its reach and coverage are broadening. Intellectual and cultural progress is a process in which modern civilization rejects ignorance both present and past. As the process drives on in depth, new resistance will be encountered, and problems will intensify. It is an arduous task to seek right over wrong, retain the genuine while discarding the false,

cultivate the good while dispelling the bad, and honor what is beautiful while negating what is ugly. Sudden progress cannot be expected
overnight, especially in moral education. "But unless you pile up little
steps, you can never journey a thousand miles; unless you pile up tiny
streams, you can never make a river or a sea."[6] Our achievement must
be accumulated gradually. Therefore, intellectual and cultural progress
is bound to be a process like water droplets drilling through rock.
Based on the above characteristics of intellectual and cultural progress, we must be willing to expend a great effort, work persistently,
and seek out good methods to promote such progress in poor areas.

Our leading officials must be both good commanders and good
practitioners. Evaluation of leading officials should consider not
only their performance in achieving material progress, but also their
performance in accomplishing intellectual and cultural progress. We
should stress in particular that leading officials should set an example.
Other officials and the people watch not only what you say, but also
what you do. If a leading official speaks against bourgeois liberalization on stage but talks with great relish about the Western multiparty
system off stage, or calls for clean government on stage but accepts
bribes and indulges in wining and dining off stage, it will be just as
the popular ironic saying goes: "He talks on stage, and is talked about
off stage." Who would believe in such a person?

To follow the mass line is a major political advantage for our
Party. We must fully mobilize the people's awareness, enthusiasm, and
creativity to participate in promoting intellectual and cultural progress.
We should launch various age- or profession-appropriate activities
welcomed by workers, farmers, soldiers, intellectuals, students, officials, and children. For example: joint army-civilian and police-civilian
efforts, selecting role models, or commend families, neighborhoods,
workplaces, villages, and towns as good examples. Promoting intellectual and cultural progress is not merely the task of one agency or
group of people, but a common cause for the entire Party and the
public. We should organize activities that please the people, rather
than putting on empty shows that bore and burden them. We should

respect the wishes of the people and actively guide them to participate, rather than rigidly forcing them to do this or that.

We should use key points to make the general case, and establish models to be promoted across the board. Dialectical materialism advocates the unification of the two-point theory and the key-point theory, which requires us to refine our leadership and improve our proficiency in promoting intellectual and cultural progress. We have to grasp both primary issues and secondary issues in the complex process of development, highlighting key points while also addressing other areas. We must establish models and promote them widely. Using this approach will help to improve our leadership and work proficiency. Ningde has had quite a few models in recent years: 178 towns and villages winning cultural awards at the national, provincial, prefectural, and county levels; 80,000 families recognized at the prefectural and county levels; and 195 individuals commended at the regional level for promoting intellectual and cultural progress. We will continue to establish models in order to foster "building blocks." Local institutions, enterprises, and millions of families in cities and the countryside are the "building blocks" of society. The purpose of establishing models and focusing on the key points is to promote intellectual and cultural progress in both urban and rural areas, and taking it to the grassroots. Optimizing the "building blocks" will enhance the intellectual and cultural level of our entire society. Focusing on the "building blocks" will in turn help establish more and better models.

Notes

[1] This refers to a mass movement that was initiated in the 1980s by the Communist Youth League, under the guidance of the Communist Party of China. The five stresses of personal behavior are decorum, manners, hygiene, discipline, and morals. The four points of beauty are the mind, language, behavior, and environment. The three loves are the country, socialism, and the Party.

[2] This refers to professional and social virtues.

[3] This refers to sweeping away cultural rubbish that polluted the social and cul-

tural environment, including obscene pornography and feudal superstitions that endangered the people's mental and physical well-being, and combating social vices, such as prostitution, gambling, and narcotics.

[4] The six evils are prostitution, pornography, trafficking in women and children, narcotics, gambling, and fraudulent activity related to superstitious practices.

[5] See Sima Qian, "Biographies of Guan and Yan," in *Records of the Grand Historian*. A native of Xiayang, Zuofengyi (southwest of modern Hancheng, Shaanxi Province), Sima Qian (145-90 BC) was an historian and writer of the Western Han Dynasty. *Records of the Grand Historian* was the first comprehensive history of China told through biographies. This colossal work spans more than three thousand years, beginning with the legendary Yellow Emperor and ending in the fourth year of Emperor Wu of Han's reign (101 BC). [Source of English translation: Guan Zi, "Mu Min (On Shepherding the People)," in *Guanzi: Political, Economic, and Philosophical Essays from Early China, A Study and Translation,* trans. W. A. Rickett (Boston: Cheng & Tsui Company, 2001), 52. – *Tr.*]

[6] Source of English translation: Xun Zi, "Encouraging Learning," in *Xunzi Basic Writings,* trans. Burton Watson (New York: Columbia University Press, 2003), 18. – *Tr.*

Enhancing Our Core Strength on the Front Line for Eliminating Poverty
– Building Rural Party Organizations

January 1990

The strong leadership of the Party in rural areas is the most important guarantee for poor rural villages to achieve prosperity. Realizing the Party's leadership in rural areas is the historical mission of the Party's rural organizations. Without strong rural Party branches, the Party's guideline, principles, and policies cannot be implemented in the countryside. And, the Party will not be able to unite its rural members, much less lead the people to grow the rural economy, develop agricultural productivity, and combat poverty and backwardness.

Since the introduction of the household contract responsibility system in rural areas, there have been less centralized production and social activities. But this does not mean that everyone has dispersed and attends to only their own matters. After the reform, we need cohesion more than ever to attract millions of farming households together to develop commodity production. Millions of farmers working together in unity is a prerequisite for getting out of poverty. When we talk of cohesion, we must also speak of our core strength; in the countryside, it lies in rural Party organizations. Whether our rural Party organizations can develop their core strength is directly related to our cohesion in eliminating poverty and seeking prosperity.

In recent years, the vast majority of rural Party organizations have withstood the tests of reform, opening up, and poverty reduction, and have become the leaders in assisting farmers to develop commodity production. A small number of Party organizations, though, have fallen behind the times and disbanded. In these places, the strength of Party organizations is gone, and the exemplary role of Party members is no longer visible. Let's examine why. First, in the past few years some Party organizations did not adhere to "grasping with two hands," giving unbalanced attention to economic reform and political work; theoretical work and Party building have been lax. In particular, rural Party organizations have not received the attention they deserve, and rural Party members have not had proper political education. Second, in our new situation, some Party members and officials in rural areas do not have a good understanding of how to let the Party organization to play its role. They believe that "production has been contracted to households, so Party branches are not needed." Some rural Party members now prefer money to principles, seek deals rather than ideals, and have abandoned their role as leading, model Party members.

The accumulation of such problems over the years makes the task before us particularly difficult. It is not a matter that can be resolved simply by issuing a few documents, convening some meetings, punishing a handful of Party members, and conducting a few rounds of Party member evaluations. We must engage in solid work and enhance our core strength on the front line for eliminating poverty through building rural Party branches and enhancing Party cohesion, with a clear guideline, a good understanding of our roles, a clean and honest membership, and improved working methods.

1. Our guideline should be clear: we Communists must conform to the common will of the people in order to represent the interests of the people. Only then can we organize and guide the people and fully develop the core leadership role of Party organizations. During the years of revolutionary war, our Party was able to unite rural people and gain their support because the Party led the people to liberation. By penalizing local tyrants and distributing farmlands to the peasants, and launching land reform, the Party brought tangible benefits to

peasants. In today's ever-changing situation, economic development and common prosperity are their common aspiration. So, rural Party organizations must lead the vast numbers of farmers to join in the cause of developing a commodity economy, promoting material and cultural progress, and forging ahead toward prosperity for all. This is the main theme for all the work of Party organizations. Rural Party organizations should make coordinated efforts to promote this theme through their work on theory, organization, Party conduct, and system building. Party organizations must make themselves a strong core to lead the people in rural areas to implement the Party line and strive for the interests of the people, so that the people will come to their own conclusion that "we must have a good Party branch to achieve prosperity."

2. We must conscientiously develop the core role of Party organizations. At the rural village level, numerous organizations – including the Party branch, village committee, Youth League branch, women's committee, people's militia, and village cooperative economic organization – are responsible for many aspects of political, economic, and social management work. The Party branches are the core leadership for them all; we can only uphold and improve this pattern and not doubt or weaken it. The key position of Party organizations is the premise for them to play their core role. We must ensure that Party organizations can truly stand at the forefront of rural socialist construction in terms of guidelines and organizational structure. In this way the Party can truly play the core role. Reforming the old rural system must not be at the expense of weakening the functions of Party organizations. Practice has proven that, as rural reform deepens, the core position of Party organizations must be strengthened. As we move forward in reducing poverty, the strength of frontline Party organizations in rural areas must be enhanced.

The village self-governance that we are currently implementing is a management method suited to rural economic reform. But we must be clear that our village self-governance is a form of socialist democracy and is under the leadership of the Party. Village self-governance cannot be divorced from the leadership of Party organizations, and we cannot place self-governance in opposition to the leadership of the Party. Only with the Party's leadership can the will of villagers truly be reflected, village self-governance achieved, and the sound development of self-governance continued.

Establishing the core position of rural Party organizations absolutely does not mean allowing them to work in isolation. Instead, as we develop the core leadership role of Party organizations, we also give full play to the respective roles of the village committee, village cooperative economic organization, Youth League branch, women's committee, and people's militia. They cooperate closely from different angles to jointly build a new socialist countryside. As with a large chorus, a Party organization must be able to be a good choir director.

3. We need clean and honest membership to strengthen Party organizations' ability to develop themselves. Without strong Party organizations, it would be unthinkable for the Party to play a core role and lead farmers in their strides forward. A person should not be afraid of being defeated by others, but rather afraid of defeating oneself. It is the same with an organization. Why can't some village Party branches speak effectively? Why don't farmers want to listen to them? With some careful analysis, the reason becomes clear: the role of those branches has already faded. Right now we must emphasize that Party organizations should give priority to their self-development. First, we must do a good job of selecting and evaluating branch members. They should be people with high political and moral standards, outstanding abilities, and sound reputation. We should do our best to ensure that Party branches comprise people who are firm in their belief in socialism and the Party's mission; who are ambitious, hard-working, and dedicated; and who demonstrate an honest and upright character. For those members who can no longer lead by example, we must timely and decisively adjust their positions. We must put particular emphasis on choosing the right person to serve as Party branch's secretary. Without a good leader, there can be no good team. Now some places are reporting difficulty in selecting Party branch

secretary candidates because there are not enough good ones due to a lack of training over the years. There are also policy issues. For example, Party branch secretaries miss time on their own production but are not well compensated because the village's economy is weak. They make contributions while serving as secretaries, but have a dim future for career development when they step down. What can we do? We should address these specific issues. We can widen our channels in the selection of village Party branch secretary candidates. Party members and officials in townships, towns, and enterprises may also serve as village Party branch secretaries for a period of time. We must take effective measures to address legitimate interests and concerns of Party branch secretaries.

Second, we must improve the intrinsic qualifications of Party members. Every Party member is a "building block" within a Party organization. A Party organization's capacity is embodied in the exemplary role of each Party member. During the previous era of people's communes[1], most rural Party members were able to take the lead, being the first to arrive at work and last to return home. We should note that today, as we develop a commodity economy and further reform, some members of our Party have lagged behind. It is not that they don't wish to accomplish something great, but rather that "the old way doesn't work, and they don't know how to do it the new way." The new era and our new historical mission have raised the sharp question of whether Party members are able to adapt. They must adapt in terms of both ideas and the ability to engage in commodity production. As Karl Marx pointed out in the *Manifesto of the Communist Party*, "Does it require deep intuition to comprehend that man's ideas, views, and conception, in one word, man's consciousness, changes with every change in the conditions of his material existence, in his social relations and in his social life?"[2] In the previous long-standing environment of natural economy, under the old rural system of being both "large and collective,"[3] our Party members more or less maintain the notions associated with the old environment and system such as being conservative, self-sufficient, inward-looking, and egalitarian. So, have these things changed yet? How much have they changed? How many new ideas and concepts have we established that are needed for developing a socialist commodity economy? But it is not enough to simply have new ideas and concepts; they need the abilities for the new environment. To engage in commodity production, run collective enterprises, and lead the way to prosperity requires Party members to possess strong abilities. There's no room for cruising along, and your work performance will say it all; just as the old saying goes, "one can tell a mule from a horse by putting them to work." The practice of many Party members has proven that those in poor areas must seriously study the basic theory of Marxism-Leninism and the Party's principles and policies, acquire scientific and cultural knowledge, learn about management, and become adept at exploring the laws governing a commodity economy. Those who do so will become leaders in socialist commodity production and lead the people to true prosperity.

4. We must base our work on reality and improve our methods. The core leadership position of Party organizations in rural areas has not changed in our new historical era, nor has the exemplary role of Communist Party members. But our work methods should change. In the countryside, moving from a "large and collective" system to a household contract responsibility system means that our work has expanded from the original several production units to tens of thousands of households. The shift from natural economy to commodity-production economy raises many new questions for us to study. Transitioning from the three-level accounting[4] under the system where "everyone eats from the same big pot"[5] to accounting based on single households means that financial incentives act directly upon individuals. All of these changes require Party organizations to stop doing things by the old playbook. We can no longer conduct our theoretical and political work by "speaking on stage while the audience listens" — a way we were accustomed to in the past. Instead, we should go out to each household and ensure that our theoretical work is well received by every farmer. We cannot sit in our office, waiting for the work reports to come in before issuing directives, but instead should take

the initiative to identify problems and help farmers resolve difficulties in their lives. We cannot merely control farmers with administrative power, but rather strive to build closer ties with them and win their hearts by doing practical things for them. In brief, we must conscientiously do our research and learn from experience as we change our work manner and improve our methods in the new situation where the economy is decentralized to each household. This is the only way to fully play the core leadership role of Party organizations.

Notes

[1] People's communes, also known as rural people's communes, were the basic unit of rural society. They combined local political mechanisms with collectively-owned economic organizations. The communes, which had integrated governmental administration and commune management with collective unified management, were dismantled after 1982.

[2] Source of English translation: Karl Marx and Frederick Engels, *Manifesto of the Communist Party* (New York: International Publishers, 1992), 28. – Tr.

[3] "Large and collective," literally "one big, two public," is an expression that summarizes the main characteristics of rural people's communes. More specifically, it refers to their large scale and high degree of collectivization.

[4] The three levels were county, township, and village.

[5] The concept of "everyone eating from the same big pot" can be traced back to the appearance of people's communes in 1958. It was closely associated with the rapid industrialization of the "Great Leap Forward." When farms were organized into cooperatives, farmers allocated resources to ensure their households had sufficient grain rations. When cooperatives were organized into people's communes, grain rations were controlled by production teams and communes, which set up "public dining halls" and "big pots." "Everyone eating from the same big pot" was a contrast to farming households who had previously prepared their food in their own "small" pots. The concept of the "big pot" brought to life the egalitarianism of the allotment system.

Developing a New Resource
– The Transfer of Surplus Rural Labor

January 1990

Reform and opening up have brought vitality to our rural economic development. With the improvement of productivity, a large proportion of the labor force has been freed from the fields, creating an urgent problem requiring our attention and resolution.

Is the continual increase of surplus rural labor force good or bad, an advantage or a burden, for an impoverished region like Ningde? I think we must engage in a dialectical analysis and address the question carefully. Good and bad, favorable and unfavorable, are not only relative to each other; one can also transform into the other. The key is whether we can grasp the essence of change in order to correctly guide it. If the rural labor force continues to be constrained as before to arable land, wielding hoe and scythe and following the slow pace of thousands of years of old farming traditions, our productivity and labor efficiency will remain low. This would not be a good thing. Conversely, looking at this massive transfer of labor from the viewpoint of reform and opening up, we are pleasantly surprised to find that we now possess a significant, precious new resource that, once developed, will create a great deal of value. We must provide timely guidance to direct the surplus labor to the development of our mountain- and sea-based resources, so we can engage in deep processing of agricultural and side-line products, develop an export-oriented economy, and seize this opportunity to push the rural economy up to a new level.

As we develop the surplus rural labor force, we must resolve the issue of direction. Some colleagues have proposed "a large number of farmers moving to the cities," but this idea is wrong. If we take a look at the history of modern global economic development, we find that, in the process of industrialization, most developing countries have faced the problem of large numbers of farmers surging into urban areas. Millions of bankrupt farmers have strained cities such as São Paulo, Rio de Janeiro, Mexico City, Cairo, and Calcutta, disrupting their careful planning and bringing about a series of urban problems, including slums, homelessness, and high crime rate. We in China cannot go this way. There is a limit to the number of rural workers who can move to cities and set up successful businesses. I think that, at this stage and for a rather long period into the future, it is unrealistic and harmful to expect cities to absorb all of our surplus rural labor force. The transfer of surplus rural labor should be consistent with the changes in the productivity requirements of the national economy, and we must take into account two realities. First, the surplus in the rural labor force is not absolute; it is relative to the amount of current arable land. For "big agriculture," we can't say for sure there is surplus labor. Second, the transfer of surplus labor is subject to spatial constraints as the countryside lacks a firm foundation and adequate food supply. A low level of education among farmers and the limited capacities of cities also add to the constraints.

So, I think the better choice regarding the transfer of rural surplus labor is to encourage local absorption: to encourage farmers to stay although they no longer work in the fields, and to enter factories but not cities. In terms of direction, we should focus on developing "big agriculture," promoting the development of mountain- and sea-based resources, and encouraging the transfer of surplus labor in line with local conditions – to farm in farming areas, do forestry work in forested areas, fish in fishing areas, and herd animals in rangeland areas. Meanwhile, farmers are also encouraged to engage in part-time businesses such as transportation, food services, and garment processing.

As the economy develops in poor areas, the development of

surplus rural labor force will be a long-term task. We should make workforce development part of our economic development plan in those areas to ensure its sound and orderly progress. At present, we must conscientiously address three problems in workforce development.

1. Developing the surplus labor force and the closed nature of small-farming economy.

The transfer of surplus labor to factories and commerce shows the openness associated with flourishing production of commodities in rural areas. It goes beyond the closed operation of small plots, breaking free of spatial restrictions. This will certainly clash with the traditional thinking resulting from the small-farming economy. For thousands of years, farmers have been confined to the land, self-sufficient but subject to the constraints of the natural economy, making it difficult for farmers to join in the life of the commodity economy. Some of them would prefer that the whole family live together on their small land, "with their faces to the earth and their backs to the sky," rather than dare to explore new business opportunities. Some would rather confine themselves to the land than get involved in other economic cooperation. Some would simply "farm for food and earn money to build a house," never thinking about producing more. These have seriously limited the scale and level of production, which in turn have impeded the development of the rural commodity economy. We must therefore free farmers' minds through education, do more to help them get rid of narrow old ideas, promote the new notion of reform and opening up, and enhance awareness of commodities, value, efficiency, and competition. Only in this way can we help release their unprecedented enthusiasm for work, open up a variety of job opportunities, and create good conditions for employment.

2. Organizing the surplus labor force and the issue of "blind migration."

The development of surplus rural labor is a systematic social project involving many aspects, and we must strengthen our guidance through planning and organization. Our existing regulatory system is ineffective, as we have virtually no idea about how, where, and when many rural residents have migrated. Such unregulated "blind migration" is likely to cause negative effects as the labor force moves. It is necessary that we plan and provide guidance for the movement of the labor force. First, we should offer guidance by providing information. Labor departments at the prefectural, county, and township levels can collect job information by reaching out to employers inside and outside of the province, and publicize such information in a timely way for farmers considering migration. Second, we should provide guidance on the establishment of business entities. Following the policy of turning "four wheels" together – supporting coordinated development at the four levels of township (town), village, groups of households, and individual – village enterprises and household industries can be set up by various means, including pooling of funds, issuing shares, and joint operations. Third, we should organize the surplus labor to engage in trade. In some townships and villages, farmers have already voluntarily formed purchase-and-sale organizations, and individual traders have emerged. But such scattered, individual efforts by farming households have serious limitations, as they will have difficulty dealing with the changes in market demand. It is necessary for administrative and commerce departments at all levels to provide guidance and take proactive and effective measures to improve the level of organization for trade activities. For example, companies and services cooperatives can be set up as rural cooperatives or joint-stock organizations to engage in diversified business. A coalition of businesses can undertake a coordinated chain process of production, processing, and sales. Purchase-and-sale cooperatives can play the role of a bridge connecting[1] commerce and rural villages.

To resolve the "blind migration" issue, we must also timely develop long-term plans and policies on the transfer of agricultural labor. With local realities in mind, we should strengthen control over the direction, volume, and speed of the labor flow, and use economic, legal, and administrative methods to manage the situation comprehensively to prevent adverse side effects.

3. The "low competence" of migrating rural labor fails to meet the "high competence" requirements of employers receiving them.

The transfer of surplus rural labor into "big agriculture" is no easy matter both in breadth and depth. This is because starting a business or joining the commodity trade business both require workers to have a relatively high education level, and the existing level of education among farmers is clearly not suited to this demand. So, we must tap the potential of surplus labor. This mainly involves work on two levels. The first is targeted pre-employment training, training existing surplus labor to become competent workers with needed knowledge and skills. The second is strengthened strategic training, making an intellectual investment by promoting vocational education at all levels, training specialized personnel, and turning surplus labor into the workforce needed for the future.

In short, developing the rural labor force is not only what the farmers want, but also a prerequisite for the vigorous social and economic development of Ningde. Deng Xiaoping has pointed out many times that, for rural areas to become well off, more than half of rural labor force would need to be freed up from farming to work in secondary and tertiary industries. We must conscientiously tackle this long-term and painstaking work, strengthen our leadership and coordination, and strive for "steady, orderly, and rational" development.

Notes

[1] This bridge helps form a tighter relationship among commerce, purchase-and-sale cooperatives, and rural villages.

How Should We Run Education?

February 1990

When we talk about education in Ningde Prefecture, there is first the question of how to assess it. Historically, we can be proud of our development of education since the founding of the People's Republic in 1949, and especially over the last decade. Before 1949 the area was a backwater, but now we have built schools, and it is not a novel thing for the children of farmers to attend university. But can we be complacent about it? I think not! As measured by the new concept of education, we must have a greater sense of urgency. What is the new concept of education? It is no longer to simply discuss education when considering education, as in the past, but rather to link education to economic and social development. We look to see whether education in this place is suited to and is promoting the development of the local economy and society. As we assess the reality of education in Ningde according to this concept of education, we cannot help but recognize the seriousness of the situation. We find that Ningde is poor when it comes to economic development, but is the education here also "poor"? It is not a bad idea to view the problem as more serious than it actually is, because this helps to increase our sense of crisis and urgency. I have traveled around to quite a few villages and have seen a lot of humble school buildings, which leave me with a heavy heart. In conversations with rural officials and farmers, I gain an even greater sense of the urgency and importance of developing agriculture through science and technology and using talent to develop our economy. Farmers are determined to become prosperous, but their lack of knowledge, science, and technology makes it difficult. We urgently await the rise of township enterprises and county-level industries. Unfortunately, everything is in place but for a shortage of talent.

We should recognize that the slow economic development of Ningde means that we lack the money to develop education, and have experienced tremendous difficulties in doing so. We should also notice that, because we have been unable to develop education well, today we are experiencing the problem of a shortage of competent personnel in our economic development. In an essay, I once discussed the Matthew Effect in education: It is more difficult to develop education in poor areas, but it is those very areas that need education the most; the less education is developed there, the poorer they become. Such a Matthew Effect is actually a vicious cycle of reciprocal causation between "poverty" and "ignorance."

So, we must view the problem of education from the high vantage point of economic and social development strategy. Ningde today is often described in five words, "old, minority, remote, island, impoverished." In this reality, to build the soft environment urgently needed for opening up and developing the economy, we must make talent the most important part of our soft environment. "Who heeds the hill's bare height until some legend grows around the hill? Who cares how deep the stream before its fame is writ in country lore?"[1] Thriving talent means thriving science and technology and a thriving economy. The economy relies on science and technology, which in turn depends on talent, and talent relies on education. Educational advancement, technological progress, and economic revitalization make up a complementary, sequential, and unified process, the foundation of which lies in education. An ancient Chinese saying is very insightful: "Respecting teachers and encouraging learning are the great foundation of a nation; promoting virtue and cultivating talent are the first service of the government."[2] We must adopt such a strategic viewpoint when considering problems, truly place education at the forefront, and strive to create a virtuous cycle in which education, science and technology, and the economy support and promote each other.

Some people say that our greatest challenge at present is insufficient financial strength to develop education. Of course we must acknowledge the weaknesses of Ningde, but we can't fail to develop education here just because our region is poor. Nor can we sit there and wait until the day we strike it rich to discuss education issues. Deng Xiaoping once said, "We should try every way to expand education, even if it means slowing down in other fields."[3] We must therefore be willing to take some time, expend some energy, and invest some money to develop education. "It takes ten years to grow trees, but a hundred years to cultivate people."[4] We can't have a "wait and see" attitude when it comes to education. Rather than arguing about whether we need better education in Ningde, we should get in gear to provide it.

With the wrong starting point, we will end up taking the wrong direction. This also applies to our work in education. As we develop education here in Ningde, it can only be based on the reality of this place.

We must be aware of at least three aspects of this reality. First, Ningde is a poor area, so education here is subject to financial constraints. Second, this area is primarily rural, so a large part of the education here should be rural-oriented. Third, education in Ningde is lagging behind in general, and many people here are illiterate. I believe that, if our education efforts are based on these three aspects of the reality, we will follow a path more in line with the needs of Ningde.

1. Balance the relationship between quantity and quality, and persist in the sustained, steady, and coordinated development of education. Since we have major financial constraints in education, we first need to follow basic national policies, create better conditions, increase investment, and ensure that the speed and scale of our efforts are both necessary and reasonable. We must also coordinate growth in quantity and adjustment in structure, and improve both access and quality. Our specific objective is to build an education system that integrates basic education, vocational and technical education, and adult education. Basic education is education in general

cultural and scientific knowledge, and is the foundation of the entire education system. Although we talked a lot about basic education in the past, there is still not enough to go around, and we need to improve its quality. Vocational and technical education is for training a new generation of workers, as well as junior and mid-level technical personnel. As Lenin said in *Raising the Productivity of Labor*, "The most reliable way to improve the production quality of workers is universal access to vocational and technical knowledge among the people." Naturally, vocational and technical education must meet the needs of Ningde's local economic and social development. It must be closely linked with helping local farmers overcome poverty and achieve prosperity. In particular, vocational and technical education should focus on practice and not simply "farming on a blackboard." We must teach students practical skills enabling them to be production experts back at home. Adult education should focus on a broad range of on-the-job training to improve the skills and abilities required of employees. Adult education is not purely cultural and technical education, but rather a comprehensive political, cultural, technical, and management education to improve the intellectual, moral, scientific, and cultural quality of workers.

There is a serious shortage of education funding in Ningde because of financial constraints; this reality will not change much in the short term. For the sustained, stable, and coordinated development of education, we must complement state-sponsored education with non-government resources. This involves engaging all stakeholders, raising funds from multiple sources, and increasing investment in education. We need suitable policies and measures on the proportion of county budgets that go to education and how non-government resources can be leveraged. We should place special emphasis on improving the effectiveness of our limited education funding. Each penny of investment should produce five, ten, or even a hundred times the output.

2. Adapt education to the development of Ningde's rural economy. Ningde is primarily a rural area, and the education must "be

imbued with rural flavor." Our goal is to have more workers who can use their knowledge to extricate themselves from poverty and achieve prosperity. For this purpose, we must integrate the development of basic, vocational and technical, and adult education. We should note in particular that, since the contract responsibility system began, family operations have been the primary mode of production in rural areas. Farmers urgently need practical technologies and techniques that help them make money soon, rather than whole sets of general theories. Skilled labor and junior to mid-level technical personnel are in popular demand for production and management. Some people may ask whether this is too pragmatic. No, it is not. What we are talking about is effectiveness. What we need is effective education for building rural socialism.

3. Focus on literacy work. We face the reality of a substantial illiteracy rate. Based on the 1985 census, 40.3% of the rural labor force in our prefecture was illiterate or semi-literate at the time. After several years of literacy work, this ratio may have declined, but probably not too much. It is worth noting that new illiterate people will continue to appear. Lenin said, "a Communist society cannot be built in an illiterate country."[5] Mass illiteracy means that many farmers can hardly acquire useful knowledge, technology, and management skills. As a result, they have very limited opportunities to achieve prosperity, while ignorant and backward customs sprout up and spread. Education in Ningde must therefore focus on literacy. Although this starting point is low, the work is essential. We cannot have an attitude that "things will be the same with or without literacy work," or that "it doesn't matter if we still have some illiterate people." We should celebrate this International Literacy Year with concrete actions. To eliminate illiteracy, we need the spirit of the "Foolish Old Man Who Removed the Mountains," increasing literacy bit by bit each year, and we'll accomplish something notable in a few years. Our literacy policy is to closely link literacy education with teaching practical skills and helping farmers prosper. Such a policy delivers immediate results – only when illiterate people understand why literacy is good for their

own vital interests will they have the internal drive to learn to read.

Notes

[1] Liu Yuxi (772-842), "The Scholar's Humble Dwelling," trans. James Black, *The Open Court*, no. 3 (1911): 187. Retrieved from: http://opensiuc.lib.siu.edu/ocj/vol1911/iss3/7. – *Tr.*

[2] See Zhu Zhiyu, "Encouraging Action," in *The Collected Works of Zhu Shunshui*. A native of Yuyao, Zhejiang Province, Zhu Zhiyu (1600-1682) was a scholar and educator in the Ming and Qing dynasties.

[3] Source of English translation: Deng Xiaoping, "Science and Technology Constitute a Primary Productive Force," in *Selected Works of Deng Xiaoping*, vol. 3, trans. the Bureau for the Compilation and Translation of Works of Marx, Engels, Lenin and Stalin Under the Central Committee of the Communist Party of China (Beijing: Foreign Language Press, 1994), 270. – *Tr.*

[4] See "On the Cultivation of Political Power," in *Guanzi*.

[5] Source of English translation: Vladimir Lenin, "The Tasks of the Youth League," in *Collected Works*, vol. 31 (Moscow: Progress Publishers, 1974), 296. – *Tr.*

The Path to Developing Big Agriculture

April 1990

I once told a *Fujian Tribune* reporter that developing big agriculture is the path we must take to fundamentally lift Ningde Prefecture out of poverty. What is big agriculture? Big agriculture is multidimensional agriculture that develops in a multi-functional, open, and comprehensive manner. It differs from traditional, uniform, one-dimensional small farming that mainly concentrates on land cultivation. Small farming is a natural economy whose goal is self-sufficiency, whereas big agriculture is a planned commodity economy aimed at the market. To transition from small farming to big agriculture entails a major change in our ideas.

First, we used to say "grains are central," while now we say "grains are the foundation of the foundation." Both sayings appear to be emphasizing the special importance of grain production, but actually they are not the same. In the past, grains were narrowly understood as cereal crops such as rice, wheat, and corn. Now, when we talk of grains, we mean all food, and this broader concept of grains has replaced the old notion of grains being the center of production.

Second, we used to talk about comprehensive development of agriculture, forestry, husbandry, side-line products, and fishery, but we overlooked their mutual relationships and mutual facilitation while pursuing economic benefits of each of these. Now we are emphasizing all-round development. This advocates operating at an appropriate scale; focusing on unifying environmental, economic, and social benefits; seeing agriculture as a systemic project and maximizing overall

185

benefits. The new notion of agricultural benefits has replaced that of individual economic benefits.

Third, in the past small farming sought to be self-sufficient, while now big agriculture is aimed at the market. It pursues the commercialization of agricultural production, and the concept of agricultural commodities has replaced that of the self-sufficient small farming economy.

We must realize that developing big agriculture in Ningde won't be easy. On this path we will be restricted in at least the following three aspects: first, our agricultural foundations are weak; second, our industrial development is slow and cannot play a major facilitating role; third, we are weak financially and can hardly meet our agriculture's needs for investment. Therefore, for some fundamental issues in developing big agriculture, we must consider Ningde's local situation within the entire country's macro arrangements. These issues include grain production, the household contract responsibility system, comprehensive development, rural collective economy, scientific and technical assistance to agriculture, and the rural service system. This article gives a basic overview of these issues except for the rural collective economy, which is discussed in another essay.

1. Grain production: plan carefully and focus on building grain projects.

Mao Zedong once said: A handful of grain puts one's mind at ease. Historically, grain production has been an issue of strategic importance in developing China's national economy. This issue is even more important and special for Ningde.

Firstly, the state of grain production in Ningde is directly related to the region's economic development. Per capita grain possession in Ningde is lower than the provincial level. Buying grains from out the prefecture is difficult. First is financial pressure. For every 50 kg of grains brought in, the province must subsidize two yuan and the receiving county must subsidize one yuan. Every year Ningde buys around 50 million kg of grains – including wheat – from outside the region or the province. This has put more strain on the already weak public finance. Second is shipping pressure. Most counties in Ningde are in mountainous regions that are difficult to access, and shipping fees are high. Third is consumption pressure. The staple in Ningde is rice, while wheat (including flour) is the main grain brought in from the outside. This runs counter to the consumption habits of ordinary people, and it costs about twice as much for them to purchase wheat flour. Therefore, if we do not resolve the grain issue properly, Ningde's economic development will be restricted.

Secondly, Ningde urgently needs to do a better job in grain production to lift itself out of poverty. According to the provincial standard, six of the nine counties of Ningde are impoverished counties, and 51 townships (towns) are impoverished, meaning that 43.22% of all townships (towns) in Ningde are impoverished. We still have not resolved the problem of food and clothing for some of our farmers, and they do not produce enough grains for their own families to live on. We can say that one basic problem of poverty alleviation in Ningde is whether people have any food and how much food they have.

Thirdly, the development of grain production will drive adjustment of the entire rural agricultural structure. One of the most basic facts is that the development of the forestry, animal husbandry, sideline products, and fishery industries relies on grain supply. Workers in these industries can do their work only when their basic food needs are met. At the same time, grains are an important means of production. The freshwater fishery industry requires enough grains to use as bait and feed, and the animal husbandry industry requires grains for feed. Also, the development of the rural food industry, feed industry, and light industry also requires a large volume of grains as raw materials. Therefore, grains are the foundation of adjusting our rural agricultural structure.

From this we can see that grain production has immense significance for the development of Ningde's economy. To bring the region's economic development to a new level, we must give priority to grain production and integrate its production, operations, circulation, and service. Good grain production relies on policy, technology, and investment, and plans for these three aspects must be formulated to support production. We must make good use of all funds and increase key investment in grain production. We must mobilize the enthusiasm of our many farmers in planting, improve the conditions for agricultural production, and focus on farmland capital construction. While improving the household contract responsibility system, we also need to establish several commodity grain bases of suitable sizes. And finally, we must focus on circulation work after grain production, establish robust circulation channels aligned to local production, and cultivate and improve the market system.

2. Household contract responsibility system: make improvement and adjustment to this system.

The responsibility system that is mainly composed of household contracts is an important result of agricultural reforms of the 1980s, and it has played an important role in arousing the enthusiasm of farmers and facilitating development of agricultural production. The reason why many farmers in Ningde have such great enthusiasm and why the region's agriculture has made such great development is intimately linked to the implementation of the household contract responsibility system. But as agricultural productive forces developed, some problems emerged in the implementation of the household contract responsibility system. For example, production models on a small scale are not conducive to farming management, and farmers tend to be interested only in short-term development. While rural reforms have seen huge successes, there is still a great need for us to clearly analyze these problems and reevaluate and consider the household contract responsibility system in two regards.

On the one hand, we must properly handle the relationship between "unity" and "independence." "Independence" refers to production and operation units that are mainly households and making full use of the initiative of individual laborers in agricultural production, while "unity" refers to relying on grassroots rural organizations to help farmers resolve problems that their households cannot resolve themselves alone. Therefore, in essence "unity" and "independence" are mutually related and not mutually exclusive. By stressing "independence" we cannot exclude all forms of "unity," and by encouraging "unity" we cannot unequivocally deny the importance of "independence." It is the combination of the two that constitutes the basic form of the socialist management system with Chinese characteristics in villages nowadays. Currently Ningde must emphasize the stability of the household contract responsibility system. As for our prefectural Party committee and government advocating for more "unity" in some places where services are weak, this does not mean "piling everything together" again, but rather means we must provide unified services to individual rural households. On the whole, neither "unity" nor "independence" means renewed restrictions on productive forces, but instead means further releasing the potential of rural productive forces. It does not mean denying farmers the right to make their own decisions, but instead means making them act more effectively on their own decisions.

On the other hand, we have to figure out how to continue stabilizing, improving, and developing the two-tiered management system of rural economic cooperation organizations. The household contract system includes the two tiers of household operations and unified collective management. These two tiers have mutually irreplaceable roles and features and also form an indivisible organic whole. If we neglect the role of either tier, we cannot make full use of the overall benefits of the two-tiered management system. Based on the actual situation in Ningde, improvements can be made in both tiers, but on the whole, the initiative in household operations has been better mobilized than that in unified collective management. There are many factors hampering the functions of unified collective management, but the key is that the collective economy in some places is weak and does not have the strength to effectively provide service. I discussed this problem in my article "Build Collective Economic Strength in Townships and Villages to Alleviate Poverty." Therefore, we must focus on gradually building up the collective economy and continually strengthen the functions of united collective management. Of course, such a buildup will take some time and cannot be rushed. Ningde is an area of mountains and seas, and we must depend on such terrain to support us. We should organize production that exploits new resources and develop vigorous township enterprises with features unique to this region. In short, we must rely on developing production and not on taking away from the household economy to increase collective power. The purpose in strengthening the collective economy is in boosting the "unity" function of collective economic organizations. This requires us to: First, we should develop a unified plan for farmland capital construction to better use and manage technology, equipment, and facilities such as farm machinery and water irrigation. Second, we need to plan for a reasonable structure of production by following both the national plan and local situation when growing crops and other plants. Third, we should build a specialized and market-oriented services system for before, during, and after production (covering production, technology, the supply of materials for means of production and sales of agricultural products). Fourth, we must manage rural reforms and development well to facilitate the stable, coordinated development of the rural economy and society.

3. All-round development of agriculture: advance agriculture on multiple levels and deep levels.

Why do we need to discuss this problem? Some of our colleagues may believe that the comprehensive development of agriculture requires both technological advantages and large investments – things available in more developed agricultural regions. In other words, in an impoverished region like Ningde, with such a weak agricultural foundation, what power and energy is there for us to make use of? At the moment let's not discuss prerequisites for the all-round development of our agriculture, and let's first answer this question: does Ningde need to comprehensively develop its agriculture? On the one hand, Ningde's agriculture has mainly focused its energy on the management of farmland for a long time. On the other hand, it has untapped mountain- and sea-based resources and product gaps that await development; many technologies, varieties, and breeds urgently need promoting. Therefore, I believe that the all-round development of agriculture is not only necessary, but extremely necessary. To bring agriculture in Ningde to new levels and broaden the path for poverty alleviation in the region, we must focus our efforts on the all-round development of agriculture.

Fundamentally speaking, to comprehensively develop agriculture in our region, we need to seek out first a broad space for big agriculture and second economic benefits from big agriculture. These are what I mean by advancing on multiple levels and deep levels, respectively.

To develop agriculture on multiple levels, we must set our sights farther and think more broadly. This means developing new resources suitable for use in agriculture, forestry, and fishery to meet the needs of population growth and social and economic development. Taking mountainous areas as an example, there is the question of how to use the land on multiple levels for forests, tea, fruits, and animal husbandry. Some places have created "green projects," providing us with good experience to learn from. Such "green projects" exploit new resources such as uncultivated mountains, slopes, lands, and tidal flats to develop multi-dimensional farming, with intensive management and professional cooperation.

Developing agriculture on deep levels involves a range of efforts. One is improving middle- to low-yield fields to increase their output. Another is improving farmland capital construction to ensure stable and high yields. Where conditions permit, we can also develop resources in uncultivated lands to make up for the losses caused by non-agricultural land use. Yet another type of effort involves strengthening water and soil conservation to improve land productivity. I believe that properly developing Ningde's agriculture on the deep levels will generate many positive effects. It will help to improve the imbalance in agricultural production, increase farmers' income, and improve their quality of life. If we develop agriculture well on deep levels, we can prove that Ningde holds enormous potential in agriculture even though it is underdeveloped at the moment.

Agriculture will change in three ways through its development on multiple levels and deep levels: first, it will gradually shift from development that mainly focuses on resource exploitation toward efficient production through technology and product development; second, it will shift from quantity-centered production to production that focuses on quality, exports, and foreign exchange; third, it will shift from small commodity production and circulation to mass-quantity production and large-scale circulation.

Developing agriculture requires large investments. Ningde is short of funding and weak in technology, and these are facts we face. However, we have plentiful labor resources, and when we combine them and put them to work we will unlock huge potentials. Irrigation and water conservancy projects, improvement of smaller river valleys in mountainous areas, forest planting, and work relief projects all require a large labor force. Surveys have shown that labor accounts for 50-60% of total investment in agricultural development projects. Therefore, one feasible path for agricultural development in our region is the comprehensive development of land resources and labor resources under the guidance of necessary state investments.

4. Developing agriculture with science and technology: guided by science and technology, supportive services are provided.

"Grain-producing projects" and all-round agricultural development, which I discussed above, rely on science and technology to make progress, improve resource utilization, and uncover potential. Given the state of affairs in Ningde with its large population, small farmland area, and relatively insufficient natural resources, we must make it one of our basic policies to develop agriculture with the help of science and technology. We must take full advantage of developments in science and technology to increase the yield per unit in crop farming and animal husbandry, and form an agricultural production system with high-output, low-consumption, high-quality, and high-efficiency.

Science and technology is a productive force. Valuing the functions of science and technology will benefit us in at least the following areas:

1) Developing and using previously unutilized resources. For example, we have so many tidal flats, why can't we use science and technology to turn them into important land resources?! With advancements in science and technology, we can also extend the use of our current resources. Such extension includes turning potential resource advantages into real resource advantages, turning resource products into resource commodities, turning initial processing of resources into intensive and deep processing, and turning one-time added value for resources into multiple added values. For example, Moso bamboo is one of our major resources. Instead of simply selling our bamboo as is, we can develop canned bamboo shoots and bamboo handicrafts and weaving products and realize comprehensive use and multiple added values.

2) More efficient use of inputs for production. This is prominently reflected in variety and breed improvement, cultivation management, and fertilization technology. First, new improved varieties and breeds can greatly increase yield with other input factors remaining unchanged or slightly increased. Second, using advanced cultivation management technology can resolve production problems that were originally difficult to resolve and save on production costs. Third, advanced fertilization technology can greatly increase the utilization rate of fertilizer.

3) Expanding the sales market for agricultural and side-line products. Increased agricultural productivity combined with poor sales will only discourage future production. For example, some places have abundant resources for producing fresh and live products, but the local market is quite limited, so it is difficult to turn this resource advantage into economic advantage. If we can use packaging that preserves freshness to ship out fresh and live products, we will be able to expand our market. Furthermore, by using advanced science and technology, we can improve the quality of agricultural and side-line products and increase their market competitiveness. This is another

area for expanding the sales market.

4) Improving the farmers' production level. When I was sent to work in Liangjiahe Village in Yanchuan County of northern Shaanxi Province in 1968, we launched a village-wide bio-gas project. As simple as it was, the prospects of applying science and technology to rural life were made clear. I still remember the smiles on the faces of the villagers when they first saw that they could cook without firewood and light lamps without oil. Practice has shown that science and technology are closely related to politics. With good science and technology resolving production and living problems, we gain support from the people.

Developing agriculture through science and technology must follow a clear direction. For us, it is guiding with science and technology and supporting with services. This effort is not only the concern of agricultural and science and technology departments, but also a task for the entire Party and all functional departments. Promoting big agriculture in Ningde must be guided by science and technology and supported by services. First, we must step up scientific research to bolster our science and technology capacity, further implement the policies that scientific institutions are allowed to do researches out of plans and the management of scientists and engineers become more flexible, and organize a large team of science and technology personnel to conduct research in agriculture. Second, we must form business service entities with multiple forms, levels, and functions; provide compensated services such as technical consulting, transfers, training, and marketing intelligence; and summarize and promote successful experiences in contracting agricultural science and technology groups in our prefecture. Third, we must establish and improve a rural four-level science and technology promotion and service network, and hire agricultural technicians to join our rural technical teams. Fourth, we must act as an intermediary for the supply and demand of technical professionals, providing guidance to technical personnel to go to farms to work and contract with enterprises and other production projects in technology industries. Fifth, we must find funding for rotating training of applied-technology teams in rural areas. We should also use agricultural schools to train farm technicians with technical secondary school degrees who are proficient in agricultural technology and will stay on and be useful in the villages, thereby cultivating a new generation of farmers.

I must emphasize that developing agriculture through science and technology must be based on education, as the development requires our farmers to have a deeper understanding in science and culture. Apart from strengthening basic education, we should also provide vocational and technical education targeting young rural intellectuals so they can become leaders in efforts to alleviate poverty and develop the socialist commodity economy.

5. Serving big agriculture: establish a service mindset, strengthen service measures.

In essence, big agriculture is a planned commodity economy. As the planned commodity economy gradually develops, farmers' reliance on specialized and market-oriented services will increase. Farmers not only need more and better technical guidance for plowing, harrowing, sowing, harvesting, crop protection, and irrigation, but more and better service regarding the supply of production means such as pesticides, chemical fertilizer, diesel fuel, and fine breeds. In addition, they need systemic services for information, credit and lending, processing, transportation, and storage before, during, and after production. We must establish a specialized and market-oriented services system and develop appropriate scales of operation to facilitate the development of big agriculture. The specialized and market-oriented services system should also integrate traditional agricultural technology services.

Big agriculture is a planned commodity economy. Our service of big agriculture should not be haphazard, and instead must have institutional assurance. Our service measures should not be simplistic, but rather offer all-around support.

We must establish a system in which the government is accountable to our farmers. All projects involving agricultural production must be based on the actual situation in the counties, townships, and villages. Clear targets must be established at all levels and confirmed in contracts, and services covering the supply of agricultural production materials, technology, and funds must be provided to the people on the ground level. We not only need to make demands of what the farmers and villages will do, but also set requirements for what services government authorities should provide. We not only need to "quantify" the production targets and contributions of farmers, but also make sure government departments and collective economy organizations at all levels perform their service duties. As long as we tirelessly mobilize all social forces available, bring all positive factors into play, and establish a specialized and market-oriented service system for agriculture, then big agriculture in Ningde will surely make major breakthroughs.

Building Collective Economic Strength in Townships and Villages to Alleviate Poverty

April 1990

I

Not long ago, I was both pleased and worried while making a rural visit. I was pleased that many farmers had begun to lift themselves out of poverty, but I was worried by the weakening collective economic strength in townships and villages. I feel strongly that, as we engage in poverty reduction, we must focus on increasing the collective economic strength of townships and villages. Otherwise, there is no basic guarantee for our entire poverty reduction effort, and it is deprived of a powerful force. We even risk losing what we have already gained in terms of poverty alleviation. As far as I know, among our prefecture's 120 towns and townships, only 20 (17%) have annual funding of more than RMB300,000 for their collective economy; 73 (61%) have between RMB100,000 and 300,000; and 27 (22%) have RMB100,000 or less. Among our area's 2,083 administrative villages, only 105 (5%) have a collective economy of more than RMB50,000, 217 (10%) have between RMB20,000 and 50,000, and 1,761 villages (85%) have only RMB20,000 or less. About half of the villages find it difficult to sustain even routine financial expenditures.

The generally weak collective economy of townships and villages in Ningde Prefecture can be summarized in four points. First, our overall level is low. The average annual self-funding for the collective economy in the towns and townships of our prefecture are only about RMB100,000, and villages average only RMB10,000, both significantly lower than the provincial averages. As an example, Jianyang Prefecture ranks in the middle of the province in terms of economic strength. Last year it required each of its townships and towns to reach a self-funding level of RMB1 million for their collective economy, and villages RMB100,000. Second, our development is uneven. Some of the more affluent towns and townships including Fuding and Gutian counties have RMB600,000-700,000 in annual self-funding, while the collective economy of the majority of towns and townships in our prefecture is extremely weak. Third, we have few revenue streams. Only a small portion of the self-funding for the development of the township and village collective economy comes from revenues generated by collective economic entities. Most comes from fiscal allocations (the majority of which comes from various industrial and commercial taxes and specialty taxes). This means that the collective economy of townships and villages lacks a strong, stable, reliable source of funding for future development. Fourth, we have insufficient capacity for sustained development. Few of our rural collective entities are starting up new businesses; most are simply carrying on existing businesses. Many of their products and equipment will soon be out of date, and new projects are few.

Why do we see such a weakening of the township and village collective economy? I believe that, over the last few years, we have neglected the accumulation and development of the strength of the collective sector in townships and villages in our guiding thought. We have not given the collective economy the position it deserves in our macro decision-making regarding poverty reduction. In particular, the distinction between unified management and simply "piling everything together" has not been well understood by some localities when implementing the household contract responsibility system. They relaxed the "unity" aspect, not unifying what should be brought together, and dividing up what should have been kept whole. The result has been that the previous "great uniformity" of the communal era has turned into "dividing up everything until nothing is left." They have gone from one extreme to the other. In some places, most of the collective economic strength accumulated since cooperatives began has vanished; what is left is not enough to be a foundation and driving force for development. Meanwhile, government departments have not provided strong administrative guidance or a correct policy orientation. For example, tax policies have been lax on individuals but strict on collectives, so the collective economy lacks the capacity for sustained growth. There has not been enough policy support and planning guarantee for funding, loans, and raw material supply. As a result, the operating mechanisms for the township and village collective economy are gradually withering away, while the pathways for enterprise development are narrowing.

Some people say that, as long as farmers are able to be lifted out of poverty, it doesn't matter if the collectives become poorer. But we say that is not right! In fact, it matters a great deal for the following reasons:

1. Increasing collective economic strength follows the socialist path and is an important guarantee for achieving common prosperity. The socialist system itself requires the establishment of an economy based on public ownership. The collective economy is an important part of public ownership and is the primary form of such ownership in rural areas. The non-public sector of the economy is a necessary supplement to the socialist economic structure, but should not and cannot become the dominant part of the economy. The collective economy is the foundation for the common prosperity of farmers, and a material guarantee as they take the road to prosperity. The healthy development of the collective economy not only provides various services to farmers, it can also play a balancing role to prevent polarization. For example, when individual income is overly high in a particular industry or sector, we can appropriately increase the amount retained for collective undertakings to prevent a widening income gap. When some farmers are still unable to extricate themselves from poverty although they work hard, the collective economy can then provide material support to them.

2. Strengthening the collective economy is the only way to revitalize agriculture in poor areas. Developing rural collective economic strength and revitalizing agriculture are interdependent and will sink or swim together. Developing our rural collective economic strength is bound to promote the added value of agricultural and side-line products, which will in turn facilitate the development of mountain- and sea-based resources, and improve the conditions for agricultural production. It will also speed up the adjustment of the agricultural production structure, spurring a continual increase in the breadth and depth of production in rural areas.

3. Strengthening the collective economy is a driving force for promoting the rural commodity economy. Developing the rural commodity economy depends on tapping the potential of family operations, which requires us to develop the collective economy continually and take full advantage of collective management. For example, we can implement contiguous area planting, which means planting major crops in a large, contiguous area on the foundation of existing family operations, which will improve farming quality and increase the effective output of the land. Having a sound specialized and market-oriented service system in rural areas is essential to developing the rural commodity economy. With a strong collective economy, we can provide effective services to household operations before, during, and after their production. We can also provide guidance for production that involves development of new resources, demonstrate agricultural science and technology, and coordinate family operations. By continually increasing our investment in agricultural production, we can also create better conditions for developing the rural commodity economy.

4. A strong collective economy provides a solid foundation for intellectual and cultural progress in rural areas. In recent years, we find that rural grassroots work is becoming increasingly difficult. The weak rural collective economy is at the root of our lack of vigor in grassroots work. A community without a strong collective economy is like a clay idol fording a river; it is hardly able to save itself. Without a strong collective economy, we are unable to undertake social welfare and

social security programs in rural areas and cannot meet the people's cultural needs. Currently in our prefecture, 200,000 square meters of dilapidated rural school buildings await repair and, in some villages, the lights are not on, no broadcasts get through, and the phone lines are dead. We advocate "bringing benefits to the locals with each term in office." If we can't address the people's problems and concerns, there is no way for us to improve the reputation of the Party and the government. If we can't solve people's practical problems in production and in life, our political work will not be convincing. Only with the continual growth of the township and village collective economy can we provide the material basis for intellectual and cultural progress in rural areas, effectively undertake collective public welfare, improve education, and cater to the cultural needs of the villagers.

II

We must focus on increasing collective economic strength in townships and villages in our effort to alleviate poverty. This is not merely a question of understanding. We can't just pay lip service to it – we must put it into genuine action. I believe we should focus on the following things:

1. Use a dialectical view of "unity" and "independence" in our guiding thought. To embody the superiority of socialism in the rural economy, collective advantages and individual initiatives should work in synch. On the one hand, the individual is inseparable from the collective. Through the collective, individual wisdom and strength are brought together to create a huge capacity for innovation. On the other hand, a collective is made up of numerous individuals. If we fail to mobilize the enthusiasm of the individuals, there will be no collective innovation. There is a dialectical relationship between the collective and the individual, or "unity" and "independence"; each interacts, depends, and serves as a premise of the other. Only when the two are integrated organically can we maintain a strong momentum to increase productivity. Neglecting either of them will result in great losses. The

problems we need to address now are: How can we fully utilize the rural economy's collective advantages without revisiting the mistakes of the past that "all are in large scale and everything belonging to the collective"? How can we effectively mobilize the enthusiasm of individual farmers without their becoming unwilling to cooperate with each other? The solution requires just the right combination of collective advantages and individual initiatives. Strengthening our collective economy does not at all mean going back to "piling everything together" as in the communal era, but rather correcting the deviations caused by neglecting unified management when contracting to households. It absolutely does not refute the household contract responsibility system, but instead improves and further develops such a system.

2. Follow the principles of using methods that suit the location and categorized guidance, be reality-based and market-oriented, and fully utilize the natural and social resources of each place. Mountainous areas should focus on developing forestry, fruit, tea, and animal husbandry. Coastal areas should start with aquacultural cultivation and work on deep processing and comprehensive resource development. We can implement three levels of categorized guidance given the uneven development of the rural economy in our prefecture.

Level 1 – Basic targets. After three years of effort, annual self-funding for each township and town will reach at least RMB100,000, and each administrative village will generate annual net income of at least RMB20,000 from collective production. These are the poverty reduction goals for the township and village levels. Each township and town in mountainous areas must secure 1,000 *mu* of high-standard forest, and each village 500 *mu*. For those townships and villages with a poor foundation which are just beginning to develop new resources, each township or town should have at least 200 *mu* of forest, 100 *mu* of tea plants, and 50 *mu* of fruit trees. Each village should have 100 *mu* of forest and 50 *mu* of tea and fruit trees.

Level 2 – Mid-level targets. Each township and town that has an annual self-funding between RMB100,000 and RMB300,000 for their collective economy will increase the funding to between RMB300,000 and RMB500,000. Each administrative village with annual collective production income between RMB20,000 and RMB50,000 will generate between RMB50,000 and RMB100,000 in income in three years. These targets apply to a large number of townships and villages with varying local conditions. That means we must focus on tapping the potentials of, and updating and transforming existing rural enterprises to enhance the benefits they deliver. We should also engage in new businesses, exploit new resources, and establish labor-intensive agricultural and industrial enterprises.

Level 3 – Higher-level targets. Some townships, towns, and villages that have better conditions than others are relatively strong in terms of the collective economy. They should raise the bar for their goals and implement a plan in which, after three years of effort, each township and town will have annual self-funding exceeding RMB1 million for the collective sector, and in each village the annual net income from collective production will reach at least RMB100,000. These places must also balance the relationship between consumption and accumulation, make good and flexible use of accumulated funds, and use multi-party financing to actively expand production.

3. Actively explore specific forms and ways to strengthen the rural collective economy. Currently, in addition to agricultural cooperatives and township and village enterprises, we also have collective and individual joint operations, collective and individual stock operations, individual stock operations, and joint operations, which are all primary forms of economic organizations in a collective economy. Examples include Yutang Village Orchard in Fuding County, where shares are issued to investors from Taiwan and to those who have contributed land, labor, and intelligence; the cooperation between Fu'an County's science and technology agencies and its townships and towns to develop integrated short- and mid-term projects to exploit new resources; and Gutian County, where accumulated voluntary service days are converted to shares in the collective enterprises and setting up collective enterprises by joining families. These experiences are worth summarizing and sharing.

I believe that we can boost our rural collective economy in the following five areas. First, townships and villages can establish various types of industrial enterprises based on available resources and market conditions. Second, government departments and enterprises can form partnerships with townships and villages to help them start up industrial and side-line production enterprises. Third, the majority of townships and villages shall continue to engage in farming, animal husbandry and processing; start up collective enterprises in forestry, fruit cultivation, animal husbandry, and aquaculture by taking advantage of local resources; and then engage in deep processing of products. Fourth, we should adjust unreasonable amounts retained for collective undertakings and fees charged to appropriate levels to accumulate more public funds. Fifth, for collective enterprises in forestry, tea planting, fruit production, and other businesses, we should resolve ambiguity and incompleteness in existing contracts, as well as contracts in which too little return is sought for the land contracted, in accordance with the Economic Contract Law.

4. Establish and improve mechanisms for accumulation and investment. With regard to accumulation, we must first improve the land contract responsibility system and gradually implement compensated land contracting so that all funds to be retained for collective undertakings will go into the public reserve. Second, we must improve specialized contract regulations and gradually solve the problems of low contract rates and declining collective income. Third, we must develop better contract goals for collective enterprises, and progressively introduce collective contracts or comprehensive risk collateral contracts. Fourth, we must implement a comprehensive plan for retaining funds for collective undertakings, where a reasonable retaining proportion is determined based on the net income of individual farmers in forestry, animal husbandry, side-line production, fishery, industry and commerce, construction, transport, and services, and the retained amount goes to the collective as a public reserve. Fifth, we must take full advantage of our abundant labor force to increase the accumulation of labor input. In short, we must actively explore ways to accumu-

late assets by developing various production sectors and services.

To do a good job in accumulating public reserves for the agricultural collective economy, we must work on developing four types of "software." The first is helping officials and the public in rural areas truly understand that increasing public reserves does not mean we want to change the current policy featuring family-based operation; instead, it will aid the further development of family operations. Once the officials and people understand this, they will then become interested in the growth of the rural cooperative economy and increase in public reserves. The second is improving collective economic organizations. Otherwise, it will be difficult to smoothly expand our economic reserves, and some existing reserves may also be lost. The third is drawing a clear line between reasonable amounts retained for collective undertakings and illegitimately imposed collections. We must manage the retained funds well and prevent losses, while respecting the legitimate rights and interests of farmers. The fourth is managing public reserves well and using them to good effect. Accumulated reserves should be used to help farmers solve urgent problems in agricultural production and to undertake public welfare projects that meet the pressing needs of farmers. We must implement strict rules regarding financial work, earn the people's trust, and resolutely put an end to embezzling public funds.

In terms of funding, we should start from our own conditions, develop a variety of economic formats, widen financing channels, and organize multi-level funding. We can implement stock, joint-operation, and cooperative ventures to attract investment; "substitute labor for funds;" and mobilize idle funds in society to develop our collective economy. We can also make use of some of our better products and existing plants and equipment to engage in horizontal cooperation across industries and sectors, inside and outside of the province and of our prefecture. We can attract investors based on the principle of mutual benefit and using dividends, product compensation, and other methods. At the same time, the departments involved at all levels should do their utmost to constantly improve investment mechanisms. The investment in agricultural from prefectural and county treasuries should increase year by year, and a certain amount of working funds should be allocated to support township and village production projects that exploit new resources. We should make sure that a significant proportion of township and village self-funding and the after-tax profits of their enterprises will go into reserves that support production. One positive factor is that favorable terms in our poverty alleviation policy will remain unchanged for two more years. We should direct a major portion of poverty alleviation funding to supporting township and village collective enterprises. Civil affairs bureaus, ethnic affairs commissions, old revolutionary base area offices, and other departments must provide necessary funding and other support for the development of the collective economy in townships and villages. Credit departments must ensure the flow of funds and adjust the structure and direction of funding to vigorously support the development of rural collective enterprises based on the principle of "encouraging growth in some sectors and discouraging growth in others, and giving merit-based support."

5. Implement preferential policies to create a favorable external environment for strengthening the collective economy in townships and villages. That includes providing concessions to rural collective enterprises on taxes, loans, funding, and raw material supply to facilitate their development. Areas where conditions permit should actively set up collective economic development funds.

6. Strengthen leadership and improve rural economic organizations to promote the development of the rural collective economy. Party committees and governments at all levels should elevate the importance of this work and place it on their key agendas. Leading officials must personally supervise work in this area and appoint a ranking official to be responsible for carrying out specific planning and implementation work. Each level should establish accountability and strengthen goal-based performance management.

Plans for township and village collective economic development should be formulated at the county level. Based on their own strengths, each should establish development objectives, strategies, and measures that are specific, proactive, and feasible. Counties and townships should target economically weak administrative villages that are yet to see progress, and implement supporting measures to ensure that these villages meet the basic targets within three years. At the same time, they should strengthen industrial planning and management, adjust the industrial structure, and prevent the unregulated projects, unchecked construction, and redundant investment.

It is necessary to improve management relations and strengthen the functionality of organizations. We must strengthen leadership team building in townships and villages, and focus more time and effort on rural economic development. First, township and town economic commissions should be established as sub-township-level agencies, to be responsible for economic development planning and management in their respective township or town, coordinate rural enterprises, and serve the township and village economy. Members of the economic commissions can primarily be from office of township enterprises, with the addition of some transferred or recruited officials. Second, we must build up village-level leadership by attracting ambitious, entrepreneurial, educated, young Party members and other able people to serve at village Party branches and village committees. We can also send determined, competent, and hardy young Party and government officials from the prefectural, county, and township levels to work at the grassroots level to strengthen leadership on their economic work. Third, we must solve the problem of compensation for rural officials. In addition to the normal allowance for village officials, each county can progressively implement a pension insurance system as their financial resources allow. Fourth, we should recognize and reward leaders of township enterprises who have made outstanding achievements. We must honor our previous policy commitment that "village officials will share a bonus equivalent to 30% of the net income in excess of the baseline of the village economy, and 5-10% of the net income in excess of the baseline of a township (or town) enterprise will be used as benefits and rewards for workers and staff."

With One Heart and One Mind, the Country and People Will Flourish

– Parting Words for the Leading Officials of Ningde Prefecture

May 1990

Time flies, and I have been working in Ningde for nearly two years. I have learned and experienced so much here. I will soon be leaving you all to take up a new position. Today I would like to say a few words as a farewell message.

Over the past two years, thanks to the joint efforts of all throughout the region, Ningde Prefecture has made achievements and realized changes. Party building has made great progress, and a stable, unified political state has been effectively maintained. Rectification and the furthering of reform are currently underway, economic development is advancing steadily, and poverty alleviation work has seen initial success. Intellectual and cultural progress has been made, all levels of Party committees have paid close attention to social governance issues, and effective measures have been adopted. There have been heartening transformations in work practices and methods, and it has become a common practice for leading officials to go among the people at the grassroots to publicize the Party's policies, make investigations, reply to people's complaints and solve problems on the spot. These changes in Ningde must be attributed to the Party guideline, principles, and poli-

This article was originally published in *Min Dong Bao* in May 20, 1992.

cies adopted since the Third Plenary Session of the 11th CPC Central Committee. This is the main reason of the changes. And, our achievements would have been impossible without the sound leadership, attention, and support of the provincial Party committee and government. They are also the results of the hard work of my colleagues here and people throughout the prefecture, built upon the good foundations laid by past prefectural Party committees and government leaders for all levels of authorities throughout the prefecture. As a Party member and leading official, I simply did what duty required of me. Hereby, I would like to express my heartfelt thanks to and sincere respect for the leaders and staff members at all levels throughout the prefecture, retired colleagues, officers and men of the garrison troops, and all the hard-working officials and people throughout Ningde who have shown understanding and support for my work.

Admittedly, the economy of Ningde is still fragile. Its basic industries still have a long way to go. Its infrastructure is incomplete. Its deficit remains high. Poverty alleviation work is yet to be brought to new levels. Party building still suffers from some weak links. Clean governance work awaits further strengthening. Social governance faces serious challenges. Some destabilizing factors remain a concern. This tells us that we still have a lot of work to do in Ningde. With a long road ahead, all of us must keep putting our noses to the grindstone.

What should we do when faced with difficulties? What attitude should we have? Do we turn tail in the face of danger? Or do we boldly advance despite knowing the challenge and welcome what is to come ready to give it our best? This is a question worth our earnest consideration. I believe that hardships and difficulties cultivate strong will and character, and when selecting officials we need to look at what kind of difficulties and challenges they have overcome. Therefore, we must not humble ourselves unduly and lose confidence.

While not ignoring the problems and difficulties, we should also see the light and hope ahead. We must see the strengths of Ningde and favorable conditions for resolving our problems: we have the right leadership of the new Party Central Committee headed by Jiang

Zemin; we have the continued attention and support of the provincial Party committee and government; we have the foundations built by 40 years of work since the founding of the People's Republic; we have the cooperation of our prefectural Party committee and government leaders and joint efforts of all prefectural and county leaders; and most importantly we have the spirit of tenacious hard-work, enterprise, and silent contributions of all the officials and ordinary people that is like "water droplets drilling through rock." Backed up by these good conditions, as long as we focus on the positive, be confident in our success, and work tirelessly, we surely will win out in the end and emerge victorious on the other side.

Even though I have seen backwardness, difficulties, and problems and have felt this burden on my shoulders during my past two years of working in Ningde, I have also seen the Ningde spirit of "feeling no shame of our predicament, working with iron will, pressing boldly forward, and striving for excellence." This spirit has moved me deeply and given me limitless strength and courage as well as many fond memories to look back on. Ningde is a place full of deep sentiments with conscientious officials and the best people one could ever hope for. I am full of confidence and hope in the development of Ningde. With one heart and one mind we have spared no effort to make this region and its people prosper, and we have no reason to not want to keep on improving it. We have every reason to believe that the "Ningde spirit" will boldly live on, and all work in this region will continue moving forward!

I have often reflected during the past two years of work, and I often discussed issues of developing Ningde with my colleagues. I have learned that to do our work well we must keep in mind the following.

Cherishing our stable situation

Only in peace can we make a country thrive and its people prosper; turmoil will bring disasters. The ups and downs of the past 40 years since the founding of the People's Republic has shown us that stability is hard fought. Without a stable political and social environment, we will not be able to advance our great causes of building the economy and the four modernizations,[1] or even complete the most basic task. The achievements from reform and opening up in the past decade will all be washed away.

As the old saying goes, "worry about danger when there is peace, then danger will never come; worry about disorder when governing, then disorder will never come."[2] When the nation is calm, we must not forget there are still dangers out there. This will give us the ability to remain disciplined in the face of danger and deal with the unexpected with full composure. In our region we urgently need to deal with industrial decline and enterprises halting all or some of their production. There are still some major issues in social governance that have not been fully resolved, and some people are still mired in the "Leftist" thinking or worship of absolute freedom. There are still some people without enough food and clothing in impoverished villages, and certain work units have still not put an end to the harmful trends of using their authority for profit and engaging in corrupt behaviors. These are all factors that affect stability in our prefecture, and all levels of leaders and departments must pay close attention to them and take up active, effective measures to resolve the problems. Even though our region's economy still lags behind other places, we can bring about fundamental changes to Ningde if the overall situation maintains stable, and if we work relentlessly in unity towards our goals.

The Party is the core force to lead our causes, and intellectual and cultural progress is an important assurance of building socialism

History has proven that just as the Party brought life-changing liberation to the people of Ningde, we must also follow the Party's leadership if we want to lift the people of Ningde out of poverty toward prosperity. Over the past two years, we have achieved some success in Party development and clean government building, but these are far from enough. We must continue our efforts to strengthen the Party while placing special emphasis on ideological and theoretical work, leadership building at all levels, and development of grassroots organizations. We must follow the Marxist guideline with regard to officials, emphasize both political reliability and competence as well as adherence to the four standards[3]. We must open our door wide when recruiting officials and not limit our selection only within the locality. We have made great strides over the past two years in fighting corruption, in particular in dealing with officials misappropriating land to build their own house in violation of law and Party discipline, abusing their power in project contracting, and engaging in graft and taking bribes. The people have welcomed and supported this. We must continue to shore up our anti-corruption efforts and build a clean government at all levels. One major task our Party committees are faced with this year is the election of deputies to the people's congress at county and township levels. This is an extremely important work. Recently, the prefectural Party committee laid down the principles to follow, and all levels of Party committees must step up their leadership in the elections. They must closely rely on the wisdom and strength of the people and make sure that leadership at all levels is secured by Marxists. During this period of time leading up to the election, our current officials must remain committed to their responsibilities, focus on the greater picture of the revolutionary cause, serve organizational needs, and work with composure.

To do a good job in Party building, we must not let up work in promoting intellectual and cultural progress for a moment. In communities, in particular in rural areas, there are still widespread feudal views and detrimental customs. Everyone should be on the lookout for the occasional emergence of feudal superstitions or disputes over mountains, forests, seas, and tidal flats. If we don't resolve these issues properly, they will disrupt social peace and unity as well as intellectual and cultural progress. Meanwhile, we should appreciate the glorious revolutionary traditions of the people living in old revolutionary base areas and recognize their deep attachments to the Party, many contributions, and few demands. I believe that these are our prefecture's most precious spiritual treasures and strengths. We should on the one hand look to root out feudal views and detrimental customs, and on the other hand promote healthy tendencies and improve Party conduct. We should strive to create a clean social atmosphere through carrying on the glorious traditions of the people in old revolutionary base areas and continuing the campaign of "learning from Lei Feng and improving work conducts."

The economy is the base and the center

Stable economic development is the foundation of stability of society, popular sentiments, and politics, and we must focus on the core task of economic development. We must hold a dialectical view toward economic development in Ningde and stay true to our policy of long-term, sustainable, stable, and coordinated development. We must both see the achievements we have made these past few years and recognize the many detrimental factors restricting economic development over the long term. Facing the actual situation in Ningde, we must throw out all unrealistic fantasies and stick to the guiding principles of "methods that suit the location, categorized guidance, acting within our means, sparing no effort, and focusing on the benefits" while solidly moving forward with our work. Leading officials at all levels must never forget: "try to hurry, and you accomplish nothing;"[4] and "going too far is as bad as not going far enough."[5] We must overcome the urge to rush ahead and restrain actions for quick, short-term benefits in economic development and instead make persevering, long-term efforts.

Within the greater national rectification effort, economic development in Ningde requires sound assessment of the situation and timing as well as a clear direction. We should give priority to two basic segments: agriculture and infrastructure. Focusing on agriculture in economically underdeveloped areas is a precondition to poverty alleviation, and it has fundamental significance for rural economic development. Agriculture is an advantage of Ningde. Our prefecture depended on agriculture in the past, and its future will depend on comprehensive agricultural development. Ningde enjoys a rich endowment of mountain- and sea-based resources, but we have not developed them enough. We must properly develop these resources, as they have major, far-reaching significance. Last year our region made great achievements in forestry work. We should solidly build on these achievements. With a few years of hard work, the mountains of Ningde will be even greener, the water will be bluer, and the people will be more prosperous. Ningde's industry will only grow powerful with comprehensive development of agricultural resources and robust growth of a processing industry that adds value to local resources. During this period of rectification, we should adjust the industrial structure and build a solid foundation for enterprises to thrive on.

Crumbling infrastructure has already become a problem "choking" economic development in Ningde. Poor transportation and energy shortages not only make it more difficult to get new projects off the ground, but also deny us from making full use of current production capacity. Therefore, we must give sufficient attention to building strong infrastructure, improving the investment environment, and creating the necessary conditions for industrial and agricultural development in Ningde and further opening up to the outside world.

The people are the driving force in the development of human history

The Sixth Plenary Session of the 13th CPC Central Committee recognized that the Party and government must maintain close ties with the people to solidify Party rule and guarantee the country's long-term stability. Looking back at history, no one has come to rule China without the support of the people. The ancient saying goes: "Good rulers love their people as parents love their children and brothers love each other. They feel sorrow when the people are cold and hungry, and distress at seeing their hardship and suffering."[6] The ancients already knew this over two thousand years ago, why shouldn't we Communists? The nature of the CPC determines that all levels of

Party officials are servants of the people. They must maintain close relations with the people, as the Party's aim is to serve the people wholeheartedly. The people are the source of the Party's power, and the mass line is our Party's basic work line. Therefore, we have no reason to depart from the people. Only when we trust the people, rely on them, and care about them, will we gain their understanding and support and will our causes win out in the end. As Lenin said, "Victory will belong only to those who have faith in the people, those who are immersed in the life-giving spring of popular creativity."[7] In recent years, some of those with weak wills within the Party have not been up to the task of governing, reform, and opening up. Corruption has crept up on us and spread, and bureaucratism has emerged, and to differing degrees this has weakened the Party's intimate relationship to the people and has eroded the people's trust in the Party. It has even allowed our enemies to sneak their way in. We must learn from these alarming facts and recognize the importance of maintaining an intimate relationship with the people.

There is even greater practical significance in Ningde to improving working practices and keeping close ties with the people. Because conditions are poor in many regards in Ningde, we are faced with many difficulties in grassroots work, and the people live hard lives. This requires us all the more to understand the situation on the ground level, check in on the people to see if they are suffering in any way, and help them resolve their practical problems. Last year we engaged in the "four grassroots initiatives" and made some achievements that were welcomed and praised by the people. We must continue our efforts in this regard and explore new and more effective ways to connect with the people.

Unity is power

The key to whether a local economy can be developed and whether the people are content in their lives and work lies in whether the local leadership team is effective. The effectiveness of this leadership team comes from the unity and collective power of its members. Unity here refers to harmony in mutual coordination and cooperation. Such leadership teamwork can be compared to that in a ballgame — the organic cooperation is the most important, and individual skills is secondary. If we overinflate the importance of individual skill without looking at overall cooperation and coordination, this will often lead to poor overall performance and impact the entire team's competitive power. How do we resolve differences between team members? Conflicts, differences, and all kinds of erroneous thinking can only be overcome through criticism and self-criticism. When team members have different views or opinions, they must have an open mind, treat each other with frankness and modesty, and try to put themselves in each other's shoes. Internally, a leadership team must recognize that unity is strengthened through criticism and superficial unity at the expense of principles must be opposed so as to make the team more powerful. Having spent nearly two years in Ningde, I feel the prefectural Party committee leaders are united, and the work environment is harmonious and cooperative. I hope that all levels of prefectural and county leadership teams will remain united as one, drum up enthusiasm, and boldly venture forth.

We should step up our theoretical studies

As J. V. Stalin pointed out, "practice gropes in the dark if its path is not illumined by revolutionary theory."[8] Our great cause at the moment is to revitalize Ningde, and we cannot for a moment forgo theoretical guidance. We are all leaders, and our work requires broad knowledge ranging across the fields of politics, economics, and society. So we must acquire a high level of theoretical knowledge. Our colleagues working in local jurisdictions will better be able to lead if they organically integrate theory with practice on a deep level.

Our work keeps us busy, and we have very few chances to step away from our regular work to concentrate on study. Therefore, we should learn from Lei Feng[9]'s renowned notion that finding time to study is like driving in a nail: just as a nail forces its way into the wood, we must squeeze in time to study, and every second counts. We should also learn from the ancient wisdom that studying is done while on three things: on horseback, on the pillow, and on the toilet. Studying must be done seriously, reasonably, and earnestly. As Confucius said, "When you know, to know you know. When you don't know, to know you don't know. That's what knowing is."[10] We must learn from books and practice with an open mind.

With lots of work to do and precious little time to study, we must focus on studying things that are important. The times call on us to study Marxist-Leninist theory, because Marxism is a summarization of the experiences of the international workers' movement. It is a theory, formed through revolutionary practice, serves revolutionary practice, and a tool used to observe all phenomena and handle all problems, in particular in the social arena. Communist Party members and leading officials who do not make an effort to study Marxist theory and methods and fail to guide their thoughts and actions with Marxism will not be able to persistently take the proletariat's stand or strengthen their recognition of proletarian thinking. Therefore, we must study the classics of Marxism-Leninism again and again and gain new insights from deep reflection on them. Now we must especially focus on Marxist philosophy, because this is a scientific worldview and methodology. As Chen Yun[11] said: Learn philosophy well – it will serve you your entire life. Learning philosophy and scientific methods of analyzing and resolving problems can keep us headed in the right direction during the complex, intricate practice of revolution and development. We must also learn economics, history, literature, and law, among other disciplines, to meet the multifaceted, multilevel needs of leadership work.

People often say that "the barracks are made of iron, while soldiers move through them like a river." It is completely normal for a person's work to change, but our causes will never stop and will always be advancing forward step by step. I firmly believe that under the guidance of the Party's basic line and correct leadership of the provincial Party committee and government, the new leaders of the prefectural Party committee will be able to unite the people of the entire region, make continued efforts, and advance all work in Ningde more quickly with better results.

This brings a story to mind: As Rabindranath Tagore, a famous poet from India, was about to return home from visiting China, a friend asked him, what have you lost from coming to China? He replied: Nothing except a portion of my heart.[12] I have the same sentiments here. Even though I am about to leave Ningde, a part of me that loves this place will stay here forever. After I leave I will still check in on how things are going here and keep doing my part to help out development in Ningde. Every positive change that comes to this place will bring me incomparable joy and comfort.

I sincerely hope that Ningde will have a better tomorrow!

I earnestly believe that Ningde will have a better tomorrow!

Notes

[1] This refers to the modernization of industry, agriculture, national defense, and science and technology.

[2] See Song Qi, *Terse Remarks*. A native of Yongqiu (modern Minquan, Henan Province), Song Qi (998-1061) was an official, writer, historian, and poet of the Northern Song Dynasty.

[3] In June 1981, the Sixth Plenary Session of the Tenth Central Committee of the Communist Party of China adopted the "Resolution on Certain Questions in the History of Our Party Since the Founding of the People's Republic of China." Adhering to the premise of revolutionization, it proposed taking progressive steps to ensure that all levels of the leadership would become younger, better educated, and more professional. The Party Constitution adopted by the 12th National Congress of the Communist Party of China officially stated that the Party would make the ranks of the officials "more revolutionary, younger in average age, better educated and more professionally competent." Since then, the "four standards" have become important principles for building the ranks of Party members.

[4] Source of English translation: Confucius, "Book Thirteen," in *The Analects of Confucius*, trans. Burton Watson (New York: Columbia University Press, 2007), 91. – Tr.

[5] Source of English translation: Confucius, "Book Eleven," in *The Analects of Con-*

fucius, trans. Burton Watson (New York: Columbia University Press, 2007), 74. – *Tr.*

[6] See Liu Xiang (77-6 BC), "The Principles of Government," in *Garden of Persuasions.*

[7] Source of English translation: Vladimir Lenin, "Meeting of the All-Russia Central Executive Committee," in *Collected Works,* vol. 26 (Moscow: Progress Publishers, 1977), 293. – *Tr.*

[8] Source of English translation: Joseph Stalin, "The Foundation of Leninism," in *J. V. Stalin Works,* vol. 6 (Moscow: Foreign Languages Publishing House, 1953), 92. – *Tr.*

[9] Lei Feng (1940-1962) was a soldier of the People's Liberation Army and a role model. He served the people wholeheartedly, was ready to help others, and was dedicated to whatever work he was assigned. He died in an accident at his post. In 1963, Mao Zedong wrote, "Learn from Lei Feng," starting a national campaign that encouraged people to emulate his selfless deeds. He is commemorated on March 5.

[10] See *The Analects of Confucius (Lun Yu).* [Source of English translation: Confucius, "Book Two," in *The Analects of Confucius,* trans. Burton Watson (New York: Columbia University Press, 2007), 22. – *Tr.*]

[11] A native of Qingpu (now part of Shanghai), Jiangsu Province, Chen Yun (1905-1995) was a proletarian revolutionary, statesman, and Marxist. He was one of the architects who laid the foundation for socialist economic development in China, and was a proven leader of the Party and the state. He was an important member of the Party's first generation of collective leadership with Mao Zedong at the core, and the Party's second generation of collective leadership with Deng Xiaoping at the core.

[12] Sisir Kumar Das, "The Controversial Guest: Tagore's 1924 Visit to China," in *Across the Himalayan Gap: An Indian Quest for Understanding China,* ed. Tan Chung (New Delhi: Gyan Publishing House, 1998), 329.

Afterword[1]

Xi Jinping

I worked very hard on my post during the two years in Ningde Prefecture along with the people and Party members there, I always felt a sense of unease. Poverty alleviation is an immense undertaking that requires the efforts of several generations. I was unable to do much in the short time I was there. In the preface to this book, Xiang Nan wrote, "I always regretted not being able to help Ningde Prefecture more than I wished to at the time." These are humble words from the venerable Party secretary. I did not fulfill my aspirations for reform and opening up in Ningde. The feeling that I still owe a debt to that region tugs at my heart. It is difficult to forget.

In this book, I have humbly ventured to offer to the public speeches and articles from my time in Ningde. This is, in part, an attempt to pay back my old debt.

During these active years of reform and opening up, when the country has been undergoing intense changes, people have rarely recorded their speeches and tended to write under pseudonyms out of fear that future readers might question their wisdom. Admittedly, against a future that will surely be very different from now thanks to the reform and opening up, what we say, write, and do today may seem to be far from perfect. The past is history. There is no need to harbor regrets.

Time is "like the passing of a white colt glimpsed through a crack in the wall."[2] Once it has passed, time cannot be recovered. We are in the midst of great changes brought about by reform and opening

220

up. Everything should be viewed with a critical eye to determine whether it will spur faster development. Anything that does not pass this test should undergo reform. One day, we may make more interesting remarks, write more beautiful prose, and do more magnificent things, but this is today. This is where the future begins. In this book, I have provided a partial record of my thoughts and actions while working in Ningde. It is my hope that they will serve as raw materials to support poverty alleviation and other worthy causes in the region. Perhaps future generations will find some meaning in this book. They can review our explorations, ponder our experiences, learn from our failures, and avoid our mistakes. The good news is that I expect this book to be forgotten. That would mean that our society has advanced quickly.

China lags behind developed countries in some areas. I will leave it to the historians to explore the reasons why. The people are interested in more urgent and practical matters. Working hard to strengthen the country, they have made a thriving and prosperous China their mission. They are dedicated to helping China escape from backwardness as quickly as possible and want to ensure that China will soon stand among the ranks of developed nations. In order to achieve these goals, everyone must agree that developing the economy is our political priority!

The 29 articles with 100,000 Chinese characters that constitute this book touch upon various aspects of different issues, but they all revolve around one theme – developing the economy. When the Third Plenary Session of the 11th CPC Central Committee was convened ten years ago, it proposed that the focus of Party work should be redirected toward building the economy. Since then, we have faced hardships and had ups and downs. We have made progress, experienced setbacks, and explored alternatives. Many people never fully understood that developing the economy is on top of our political agenda. They never could shift their thinking. After reforms were put into practice, however, the proof could not have been any clearer. The superiority of socialism is most fully manifested in the liberation of productive forces, the rapid building up of our national strength, the great improvement to people's lives, and the increased contact we have with the outside world. China's success can be attributed to our early emphasis on the importance of developing the economy, our determination to take quick action, and our foresight to firmly establish industries. China has become an influential country with a firm stance and a resounding voice on the world stage. Our dedication to reform and opening up has led to economic development that is the envy of the world.

Socialism is an unprecedented undertaking. Generation after generation have attempted to explore socialism with varying degrees of success. There have been mistakes and even failures. Yet, people try and try again until they succeed. This infinite cycle is the only correct way to achieving socialism.

During his tour of southern China this year, Deng Xiaoping said, "Practice is the sole criterion for testing truth. ...there is one thing I believe in: Chairman Mao's principle of seeking truth from facts. That is the principle we relied on when we were fighting wars, and we continue to rely on it in construction and reform. We have advocated Marxism all our lives. Actually, Marxism is not abstruse. It is a plain thing, a very plain truth."[3]

Deng Xiaoping also pointed out, "We should be bolder than before in conducting reform and opening to the outside and have the courage to experiment. We must not act like women with bound feet. Once we are sure that something should be done, we should dare to experiment and break a new path. That is the important lesson to be learned from Shenzhen."[4] "If we don't have the pioneering spirit, if we're afraid to take risks, if we have no energy and drive, we cannot break a new path, a good path, or accomplish anything new."[5]

I am advocating action. Practice trumps knowledge because practice is based on action. Instead of fearing we will say the wrong thing, we should worry about suffering from a "poverty mentality" that prevents us from envisioning bolder ways to implement reform and opening up. Instead of fearing we will do the wrong thing, we should worry about experiencing "poverty thinking" that blocks us from taking stronger action to conduct reform and opening up.

When I was leaving Ningde for my new post in Fuzhou two years ago, *The People's Daily* happened to publish a report that Ningde had been lifted above the poverty line. Friends happily called to share the news, but I did not feel any sense of relief. Compared with our ideals, our goals, and the true meaning of "free from poverty," I knew that helping lift people above the poverty line was only a start. Yet I am convinced that "one hundred, one thousand, and even one million, all start out as one." If we continue to steel ourselves against hardships, remain dedicated to the cause, make persistent efforts, and refuse to yield in our struggle, we can cast off the yoke of poverty permanently.

The title of this book is *Up and Out of Poverty*. Its significance lies first and foremost in uprooting our "poverty mentality" and "poverty thinking." We must eradicate the "poverty" that exists in our minds before we can eradicate it in the regions we govern, before we can help the people and the nation out of poverty and embark on the road to prosperity.

Notes

[1] The text was taken from the afterword of the Chinese edition.

[2] Source of English translation: Zhuang Zi, "Knowledge Wandered North," in *The Complete Works of Zhuangzi,* trans. Burton Watson (New York: Columbia University Press, 2013), 181. – *Tr.*

[3] Source of English translation: Deng Xiaoping, "Talks in Wuchang, Shenzhen, Zhuhai and Shanghai," in *Selected Works of Deng Xiaoping*, vol. 3, trans. the Bureau for the Compilation and Translation of Works of Marx, Engels, Lenin and Stalin Under the Central Committee of the Communist Party of China (Beijing: Foreign Language Press, 1994), 370. – *Tr.*

[4] *Ibid.,* 360. – *Tr.*

[5] *Ibid.* – *Tr.*

图书在版编目 (CIP) 数据

摆脱贫困：英文 / 习近平著.

-- 北京：外文出版社；福州：福建人民出版社，2016

ISBN 978-7-119-10556-7

I. ①摆… II. ①习… III. ①习近平 – 讲话 – 学习参考资料 –

英文②社会主义建设 – 福建 – 文集 – 英文 IV. ① D2-0 ② D675.7-53

中国版本图书馆 CIP 数据核字 (2016) 第 263602 号

摆脱贫困

习近平　著

© 外文出版社有限责任公司

中非合作论坛中方后续行动委员会秘书处

福建人民出版社有限责任公司

外文出版社有限责任公司　福建人民出版社有限责任公司　出版发行

（中国北京百万庄大街 24 号）

邮政编码：100037

http://www.flp.com.cn

环球东方（北京）印务有限公司印刷

2016 年 11 月（小 16 开）第 1 版

2016 年 11 月第 1 版第 1 次印刷

2019 年 8 月第 1 版第 6 次印刷

（英文）

ISBN 978-7-119-10556-7

11000 （精）